V. - Stars twinkled
flying clouds
flash of lightning.

h - talk - wood -
marval projection
muscles -
horses prick ears

P - chopping of tree
muff

# Berkeley Square

## A PLAY IN THREE ACTS

BY
### JOHN L. BALDERSTON

*(The plot suggested by Henry James' posthumous
fragment, "The Sense of the Past." The Author
also acknowledges the invaluable assistance of
J. C. Squire)*

SAMUEL FRENCH, INC.
25 WEST 45TH STREET, NEW YORK, N. Y.
811 WEST 7TH STREET, LOS ANGELES, CALIF.
SAMUEL FRENCH, LTD.
26 SOUTHAMPTON STREET, STRAND, W.C.2, LONDON

13384

# "BERKELEY SQUARE"

## ALL RIGHTS RESERVED

Printed in the United States of America by
THE RICHMOND HILL RECORD, RICHMOND HILL, N. Y.

# DESCRIPTION OF CHARACTERS

MAID: WILKINS, *the Maid. Wears a blue-grey dress with frilled mob-cap.*

TOM PETTIGREW: *A youth in his twenties, clothed as a town buck of the period. He has aristocratic features. His mouth normally twisted into a sneer; he is naturally coarse, brutal, disagreeable under the veneer of good breeding.*

KATE PETTIGREW: *Twenty-five, dressed fashionably, cool, competent, handsome, self-assured.*

LADY ANNE PETTIGREW: *Wears the high wig in fashion a few years earlier. She is fifty, stout, high-nosed, determined; rather a dragon.*

MR. THROSTLE: *A dandified, fussy, precious little man of forty odd.*

HELEN PETTIGREW: *A girl of about twenty. Simply dressed. She has a wistful, sensitive face. She is in all respects a contrast to her polished, worldly sister.*

THE AMBASSADOR: *Elderly, distinguished, suave, urbane, sensitive.*

MRS. BARWICK: *An elderly housekeeper, dressed in grey with a white apron.*

PETER STANDISH: *Twenty-six. Wears a long, black dressing-gown. Nervous and sensitive. Needs his hair cut. His manner jumpy and feverish.*

MARJORIE FRANT: *An attractive girl in the late twenties, dressed with sensible good taste.*

MAJOR CLINTON: *A good-looking soldier of thirty.*

MISS BARRYMORE: *A smart girl of the period. Aged twenty.*

THE DUCHESS OF DEVONSHIRE: *Beautiful and distinguished.*

LORD STANLEY: *Under-Secretary of the Foreign Office, a man of about fifty, who wears an order.*

THE DUKE OF CUMBERLAND: *Elderly, many-chinned, amiable. He wears the Garter with ribbon and star.*

3

The following is a copy of program of the first performance of "BERKELEY SQUARE," as presented at the Lyceum Theatre, New York, N. Y.:

GILBERT MILLER & LESLIE HOWARD'S
Production of
BERKELEY SQUARE
A Play in Three Acts
*By* JOHN L. BALDERSTON

## THE CHARACTERS
(In the order of their appearance)

MAID ............................................*Irene Howard*
TOM PETTIGREW ...................... *Brian Gilmour*
KATE PETTIGREW ...................... *Valerie Taylor*
THE LADY ANNE PETTIGREW ............ *Alice John*
MR. THROSTLE ........................ *Traver Penna*
HELEN PETTIGREW ............... *Margalo Gilimore*
THE AMBASSADOR .................. *Fritz Williams*
MRS. BARWICK .................... *Lucy Beaumont*
PETER STANDISH ................... *Leslie Howard*
MARJORIE FRANT ................... *Ann Freshman*
MAJOR CLINTON ................. *Charles Romano*
MISS BARRYMORE .................... *June English*
THE DUCHESS OF DEVONSHIRE ...... *Louise Prussing*
LORD STANLEY .................... *Henry Warwick*
H.R.H. THE DUKE OF CUMBERLAND....*Robert Greig*

*The action throughout takes place in the morning room
of a house of the Queen Anne period in Berkeley
Square, London, in the years 1784 and 1928.*

## SYNOPSIS OF SCENES

### ACT I
SCENE I: *Five o'clock, October 23rd, 1784.*
SCENE II: *Five o'clock, October 23rd, 1928.*
SCENE III: *Continuous with Scene I.*

### ACT II
SCENES I AND II: *Night—a few days later, 1784.*

### ACT III
SCENE I: *Afternoon in 1784, a week later.*
SCENE II: *Continuous with Scene I, but in 1928.*

# Berkeley Square

## ACT ONE

<small>Scene I:</small> *October the 23rd, 1784.*

*The morning-room of a Queen Anne house
in Berkley Square. It is panelled and painted
a creamy white. There are two long recessed
windows at the back, with pelmets and curtains
or rose-colored Italian brocade that fall to the
window-seats. They look out into the trees of
the enclosed garden, now drenched with rain.
The back cloth shows houses across the Square.
In the Right wall, well down stage, a wide door
(which is hinged down stage) opens on stage
(inwards), and above this a tall Queen Anne
walnut writing-bureau, closed, stands against the
Right wall back stage, with a needlework-cov-
ered walnut stool in front of it. Between the
door and the writing-bureau, a walnut chair. In
the Centre panel of the rear wall hangs a tapestry; under this, a delicately modelled gilt console table, with a Chelsea group upon it. An
armchair a little to the front and Right of the
table. Large fireplace, set at an angle across the
corner between the L. window and a door in
the Left wall, has bolection moulding around
the fire, and a painted landscape let into the
panel above. Small table, folded, against the
back wall between L. window and fire; and on
each side of the double doors stands a walnut*

5

*cabriole-leg chair. Mirror and bell pull on the*
*wall between fireplace and door; low walnut*
*stool before fireplace. A small settee is placed*
L.C.; *to the Right of this a walnut cabriole-leg*
*table, with small drawers, used as a work-table.*
*Occupying the Centre of the stage, a section of*
*an oval rug, yellow, with a Chinese design in*
*blue and rose. Parquetry stage cloth on part*
*of floor not covered by rug. The room is lit by*
*five glass sconces of two lights each, one between*
*writing-bureau and door, one to the* R. *of the*
R. *window, one to the* L. *of* L. *window, one on*
*each side of the double door. (The candles, for*
*convenience in later stage directions, may be*
*numbered from* L. *to* R., *1, 2, 3, 4, 5, 6, 7, 8, 9,*
*10.)*

AT RISE: *There is a sound of rain at rise of curtain.*
*Five full deep notes are heard from a grand-*
*father clock—offstage, on the landing outside*
*the door* R. *It is dusk. The fire is burning.*
*Candles 1, 2, 3, 4 and 5 are lit as the CURTAIN*
*rises.*
     *The window curtains are open and the* R. *win-*
*dow is open.*
     WILKINS, *the Maid, wearing a blue-grey dress*
*with frilled mob-cap, is discovered with taper*
*lighting candle 6. She lights candles 7, 8, 9 and*
*10. She blows out the taper, and as she is draw-*
*ing the curtains the SOUND of a horse's hoofs*
*and wagon rumble is heard. The horse stops*
*outside. She hurries out* R. *Pause. In a few mo-*
*ments she re-enters* R., *carrying a letter in her*
*hand.* TOM PETTIGREW *follows. He is a youth*
*in his twenties, clothed as a town buck of the*
*period. He has aristocratic features. His mouth*
*normally twisted into a sneer; he is naturally*
*coarse, brutal, disagreeable under the veneer of*

*good breeding. He is very slightly tipsy. The* MAID *is crossing to* L.

TOM. What have you there?

MAID. (*Stopping* C. *and turning to him with a familiar grin*) For her ladyship, sir.

TOM. (*Extending his hand*) Give it to me.

MAID. (*Hesitates*) But 'tis for her ladyship.

TOM. (*Scowling—comes to her* C.) Give it to me! (MAID *reluctantly lets him take the letter. He stoops to kiss her, his* L. *arm around her.*)

MAID. (*Shrinking*) No, please, Mr. Tom!

TOM. (*Laughing*) Gad's life, Wilkins, when did you turn prude?

MAID. I told you I'm to be married, sir.

TOM. Ay, but to whom, my love? Some lusty great footman, what? (*As thought strikes him*) And if we found him—(*Leers at her*)—we could tell him something.

MAID. (*Terrified—almost in a whisper*) Oh, Mr. Tom, you'd never——        (RAIN *Dies Out.*)

TOM. (*Seizing her*) We're more reasonable now, ain't we? (*Enter* KATE PETTIGREW, L., *carrying needlework. She is twenty-five, dressed fashionably, cool, competent, handsome, self-assured. She stops at door.* TOM *releases* MAID) Damme, you shouldn't slink about. (*Moving up stage* L.C. KATE *makes a gesture of dismissal to* MAID, *who exits by door* R., *and advances* C. *via above settee.*)

KATE. (*Contemptuously*) Are not maids difficult enough to find, at the beggarly wage we can afford, without your making the keeping of them impossible?

TOM. (*Comes down again to* R.C., *trying to recover his poise*) 'Tis me you should thank, Kitty, that they seek our employment at all.

KATE. Foh! Your tastes are those of a stable-boy! (*Turning away toward fire.*)

TOM. Your tongue is worse than Helen's great

staring eyes when she looks through a man. An agreeable pair of sisters! I'll not endure it. While my father's at sea, am I not his deputy here?

KATE. *(Laughs contemptuously)* A pretty deputy! I hope you'll repeat that remark to our mother. *(Turns away* L. *and sits settee—continues her sewing.)*

TOM. And why not, pray? Where is her ladyship?

KATE. *(Puts her work in* L. *front drawer of small table* C. *by* L.*)* You had best avoid her. Your latest follies have set her beside herself.

TOM. *(Importantly)* She will forget such trifles when she hears my news.

KATE. *(Mockingly)* Is it so important? Has Miss Sinclair taken pity upon you at last?

TOM. 'Tis a lie! I never asked her.

KATE. How many malicious tongues there are in town—'tis said she is the sixth to refuse you.

TOM. *(Moving* R.*)* Damn them all, no woman nowadays will look at a man without money. *(Preening himself—sits on stool before desk, facing front)* —until after she's married a man who's got it!

KATE. If you realize you've no money, why must you gamble as though you'd a fortune?

TOM. *(Mysteriously)* Ah, Fortune! Perhaps Fortune is but now knocking at our door. I come as Fortune's herald.

KATE. *(Facing him* C.*)* I *thought* you were tipsy.

TOM. If Helen were here she'd interpret my oracle, and not carp like a Covent Garden orange wench.

KATE. *(Curious but haughty)* Why so classical today? First a herald, now an oracle?

TOM. Helen could read my riddle. Helen could see through the wall with those damned eyes of hers —and what d'you think she'd see? Fortune approaching this house, now, in the flesh. Fortune—*(Rises— crosses to down* R.C.*)*—wearing breeches, no doubt very badly cut. *(Teasingly)* Now. Three guesses, Kate.

KATE. *(Intensely excited; rises; crosses to L. of him)* Is he—has Cousin Peter arrived from America?

TOM. Faith, you have guessed it in one!

KATE. *(Turns, walks L., puts sewing in drawer of table C.)* If you are the first Pettigrew he's met, we are unfortunate!

TOM. *(Crosses up R. toward window)* He has not had that honor.

KATE. *(Turning, impatiently)* Then how do you know he's in London?

TOM. Met Bill Clinton in St. James's Street not an hour since. He came with him from New York in the *General Wolfe.* (KATE *starts to go out L.*) So you've no interest in my further news? *(Waves letter tantalizingly in his R. hand.)*

KATE. *(Turning)* From him?

TOM. *(Scrutinizing it at arms' length)* I judge so!

KATE. *(Goes R.; holds out hand)* Give it to me!

TOM. *(Affecting to be shocked. Puts letter behind him)* When 'tis directed, as is proper, to her ladyship?

KATE. *(Turns, crosses to above double doors and pulls bellcord)* And you have kept it all this time?

TOM. I thought to find your Yankee already here. He can't be so eager as his letters have made you suppose.

KATE. He sends an intimation before him, as any gentleman would.

TOM. *(Walks L. to her, behind settee. Sneering)* Gentleman! From New York! Now look'ee, Kitty. Hook this Colonial and there need be no more talk of beggary in this family. *(The MAID enters R.)*

KATE. Wilkins! Find out her ladyship and give her this letter. (TOM *gives* MAID *letter* C. MAID

*exits* L. *via below settee.* TOM *sits before desk again.*)
I know what you've in mind. He is not to know of
your debts.

TOM. D'you think all the benefits from this arrangement are to be yours?

KATE. (C.) I know of no arrangement.

TOM. I suppose there's been no suggestion of a
settlement of fifteen thousand pounds?

KATE. I've not said I'll have him.

TOM. *(Dryly)* You will.

                                        *(WARN Clock.)*

*(Enter* LADY ANNE L., *carrying letter open. She
    wears the high wig in fashion a few years ear-
    lier. She is fifty—stout, high-nosed, determined;
    rather a dragon. Comes above table to* R. *of
    them.)*

LADY ANNE. Kate! Thomas! He's arrived.
Cousin Peter is in London! *(Waves letter.)*

KATE. *(Comes to her quickly as she turns around
table and sits on* R. *of settee.* TOM *also comes to them
above table)* Read it, ma'am! (KATE *sits by her
mother.* TOM *leans over back of settee.)*

LADY ANNE. *(Fumbles with lorgnette)* Let me
see. Ah, "October 23rd, 17 and 84. Honored madam.
Having arrived within the hour——"

TOM. Where'd he send this from?

LADY ANNE. *(Fumbles again and peers)* The
Blue Boar in Jermyn Street.

TOM. Lodges in that old stable, when he's ten
thousand a year.

KATE. Go on, ma'am.

LADY ANNE. *(Elaborate)* "—within the hour,
traveling by post from Plymouth, I make haste to
dispatch you this intimation that I shall do myself
the honor to wait upon yourself, my fair cousins, and
Mr. Pettigrew, at a half after five this evening, in

Berkley Square. I subscribe myself, Madam, your most obedient cousin and humble servant, Peter Standish. To the Lady Anne Pettigrew."

KATE. *(Rises)* Our cousin's letter is well-bred. *(TOM crosses down R.C.)*

LADY ANNE. Mr. Standish's letters from New York have already vouched for his parts.

TOM. *(Crosses down R.)* And Messrs. Baring's discreet replies, for his substance.

LADY ANNE. *(Surveying KATE thoughtfully)* You look charming, my child.

TOM. *(Looks at her appraisingly)* Such blushes, too. Art or nature?

KATE. *(Rises; moves slightly to L.)* More natural than wit in you.

TOM. Your husband will find you sharp of tongue, my lass. *(CLOCK outside on landing strikes once. TOM moves R.; looks at his watch.)* A quarter after five o'clock. The cavalier should be here ere long.

LADY ANNE. *(After a moment's thought. Rises; comes C.)* Tom, you will greet him below and bring him here. *(To KATE)* And you will welcome him on my behalf.

KATE. *(Turns to her mother and comes to table L.C.)* Not—alone? Surely you will present him to me?

TOM. My sister fears that she would make herself cheap.

LADY ANNE. Hold your tongue! *(Comes to KATE at table)* You will do as I tell you. When I return I shall know—— *(Crosses and sits L. of settee.)*

TOM. The baggage is bashful! *(KATE pats sewing in center drawer of table C.)* Where learnt you this trick, Kate? Gad's blood, if only he'll have you!

LADY ANNE. He wants an English wife, and he commends Kate's miniature. Where else could he aspire to such a connection?

TOM. Our mother is ingenious. If you fail to

please in person as you did by post, there's still another daughter——

LADY ANNE. What insolence is this?

TOM. *(A bit cowed, but pressing on, strolls across stage; sits in chair* L. *downstage)* My poor friend Throstle's fifteen hundred a year is scarcely to be set against ten thousand——

LADY ANNE. Enough of your crude jesting. You will know whom Helen is to marry.

KATE. But Helen's disposition, ma'am. *(Sits by mother on* R. *of settee.)*

LADY ANNE. You may safely leave Helen's fancies to me, and trust her mother to act in her interests.

TOM. *(To* KATE*)* Ay, and in ours too. And as for your prejudice against my friend Throstle——

KATE. Your friend, while you can borrow from him!

TOM. Gad, even tailors have to be paid somehow.

KATE. The disgusting little man!

LADY ANNE. Kate!

TOM. What's wrong with him? Teeth none too good, perhaps, but an artist, a man of parts, not without generosity.

KATE. Such as you hope to find in Mr. Standish! *(To* LADY ANNE*)* He'll ruin everything! *(To* TOM*)* I wish you'd go racing at Newmarket for the week.

TOM. And who then would dry-nurse Master Colonial?

LADY ANNE. You are not to say Colonial. The Colonists are now independent.

TOM. Yankee puppy, then.

LADY ANNE. Peter Standish is your cousin!

TOM. What was his father? A fur dealer, a tradesman!

LADY ANNE. His grandfather built this house.

TOM. And lost his money—fled to America with

the scum o' the country and married God knows
whom there.

KATE. Dry-nurse indeed! You think to find him
drink, women and cards, so that he pay for yours.

TOM. I shall. But I will get you your husband.

LADY ANNE. You grow offensive, sir!

KATE. And is it likely that such a man as our
cousin will put himself in your hands?

TOM. Such a man! His polite letters have foxed
you, Kitty.

LADY ANNE. What do you know of him?

TOM. (Mischievously) Bill Clinton told me he's
a devil of a temper. Got cashiered from the rebel
army for insubordination.

LADY ANNE. (Anxiously) Every woman likes a
man of spirit. What else did Clinton say?

TOM. (Laughing) That he can drink any two
men of us here under the table. That the mothers
in the Yankee villages locked up their daughters
when Captain Peter Standish was looking for bil-
lets.

LADY ANNE. (Angrily, anxiously looking toward
KATE) These are monstrous lies!

KATE. He thinks to disturb me, ma'am, with absurd inventions.

TOM. (Indignant) Inventions! (Laughs again)
I leave those to your Yankee! Clinton says he's always inventing things——

KATE. (Indifferently) Our cousin has written me
of his hobbies. (TOM rises; moves to R.C.)

TOM. (To LADY ANNE, changing his tone) I had
thought to put him down at White's, ma'am. (Rises,
embarrassed; strolls behind settee, hands behind
back.) We might lighten this load of dollars there.
But at the moment that attenion is beyond me.

LADY ANNE. (Suspiciously) Indeed? And why?

TOM. (His back to them) Because of a slight put
upon me by the committee.

KATE. *(Turning and facing to* L.*)* He's been posted at his club.

TOM. *(Sheepishly, coming around before small table)* If I am to show him proper civility, I must beg a hundred pounds of you, ma'am.

LADY ANNE. You had fifty but Tuesday!

KATE. Gambling again!

TOM. I'm a gentleman and do as my equals. Am I to parade our wretched poverty before the town?

KATE. Need you scatter months of our pin money in an evening?

TOM. *(To* KATE*)* Think you I'd grudge you a hundred pounds had I a settlement of fifteen thousand all but in my hands?

LADY ANNE. You are insupportable. I know not where to turn for money.

TOM. *(Strolls* R.*)* After this once, ma'am, I'll not need to trouble you more.

KATE. He means to rob our cousin.

TOM. *(Snarling, turning on her)* Rob! How dare you!

KATE. Rook, then.

TOM. *(A step toward her)* D'you mean I play unfairly, wench?

*(Enter* MAID R.*, standing above the door—announcing.)*

LADY ANNE. Kate! Thomas!

MAID. Mr. Throstle, your ladyship.

*(*THROSTLE *enters* R. *A dandified, fussy, precious little man of forty odd. The* MAID *goes out after he has passed her.* LADY ANNE *and* KATE *rise Bows and curtsies exchanged.)*

THROSTLE. *(Moves* C.*)* Your servant, Lady

Anne! Miss Pettigrew! Your servant, sir! *(Bowing to* TOM. LADIES *resume seats.* TOM R., *up stage.)*

LADY ANNE. *(With a smile and a wave of her hand toward window)* Even the rain cannot keep faithful Mr. Throstle away. (TOM *moves to* R. *and sits in chair by door* R.; *reads newspaper.)*

THROSTLE. Madam, I learned at the Bull that a certain coach has borne a precious freight to London——

LADY ANNE. *(Smiling at him)* She will be down directly, sir; she stays only to change her gown.

THROSTLE. Miss Helen indeed comes first in my thoughts, even when my curiosity is so lively respecting your Croesus of a cousin—whose arrival——

TOM. *(Puts down paper)* Does anything ever happen that you don't hear of it in the instant, Throstle?

LADY ANNE. He'll be with us at any moment now.

THROSTLE. *(Still standing slightly back* C.*)* Mr. Standish, I gather, has never been in England? If I can be of assistance, in effecting introductions——

LADY ANNE. Oh, sir, we shall indeed make bold to enlist your help.

TOM. And we'll need it, Throstle! If only he'll imitate his better, but these Yankees! 'Twan't worth our trouble to catch and hang the lot, so they say they won the war!

*(Enter* HELEN L.; *crosses to* C. *via above settee. A girl of about twenty. Simply dressed. She has a wistful, sensitive face. She is in all respects a contrast to her polished, worldly sister.* THROSTLE, *who has been looking toward* TOM, *turns, stopping* HELEN *as she is about to come around small table to the other ladies.* HELEN *about to speak to* KATE *when she is stopped by* THROSTLE *speaking to her.)*

LADY ANNE. You are not to mention the late war with America!

TOM. You don't know these Yankees. 'Twon't be I who'll mention it.

THROSTLE. *(Kissing her hand)* Your most devoted, faithful slave, now as always, dear Miss Helen.

HELEN. *(Curtseys R. of table C.)* I am your servant, sir.

THROSTLE. The week of your absence has been to me a desert.

HELEN. *(Absently)* Thank you, sir.

*(WARN Coach and Hoofs.)*

KATE. *(Bursts out to HELEN)* Cousin Peter's in London!

HELEN. *(Phrased as a question, she conveys that she knows)* He's on his way to us now?

TOM. Helen! Observe Kate's maidenish agitation! Mother has contrived that she's to meet him first, and alone.

HELEN. *(Whose back has been turned to TOM)* Mother! What *will* Cousin Peter think?

LADY ANNE. *(Severely)* Think? What should he think? Our cousin has written, Mr. Throstle, that he would buy a town house, a country estate——

TOM. And a wife!

HELEN. Oh, Tom!

THROSTLE. *(Interposing)* The lady upon whom Mr. Standish prevails then need not exchange our civilized society for Mr. Washington's crude democracy?

*(COACH and Hoofs.)*

LADY ANNE. What Miss of quality would leave London for the Colonies?

TOM. Now who said Colonies?

HELEN. *(Still standing just behind R. end of settee, where THROSTLE stopped her)* I hear a coach.

"BERKELEY SQUARE"

Act I, See Page 10

*(NOISE OF COACH STOPS.* Tom *hurries to window* R.; *draws back curtains.* Kate *and* Lady Anne *to window* L., *peer through curtains, looking out.* Throstle *moves to* Helen *as if to take her hand. She has been looking straight ahead; she turns, looks at him. He turns from her, passes below settee, taking snuff.)*

Lady Anne. *(At window Left)* 'Tis he! Look, Kate! A most elegant young man!

Tom. *(With faint sneer)* His back is most elegant.

Lady Anne. *(Turning)* Now, Tom, downstairs to him.

Tom. Good luck with your savage, Kate!

Kate. Savage or not, there's to be no sneering.

Tom. *(Turning at door* R., *jokingly to* Kate*)* You'll need those blushes now. *(Exits* R.*)*

Lady Anne. *(Crosses almost to door* L.*)* Come, come into the drawing-room. *(She waves* Throstle *out* L. *He goes out, leaving door open.)* He is the handsomest man, Kate!

Kate. *(Hysterically; crosses to above settee)* This is too much, ma'am! Would you have me sell myself to pay our debts?

Lady Anne. *(Coming back slightly to* Kate*)* Kate, dear Kate, I meant no such thing. *(NOISE of coach turning; sound of coach and hoofs fading in the distance.)* Come, Helen! *(Hurries from the room. Exit* L.*)*

Kate. *(Turns to* Helen*)* Oh, Helen! *(Standing above and Centre of settee)* Mother presses me so. Oh, Helen, will he be as we pictured him?

Helen. *(Playfully, standing* C.*)* How indeed can I know? I've not even seen his back.

Kate. Tom has heard dreadful things——

HELEN. *(A step toward her)* I believe he will be —all that you could wish for.

KATE. Then he may not care for me!

HELEN. *(Crosses impulsively to her)* He will, dearest, he will!

*(WARN Shadow Light.)*

KATE. *(Both above settee)* Why must Mother take it so hard——

HELEN. I know. But only be yourself, Kate. *(Crosses to door L. Faces KATE when at door and speaks in tenderly chaffing tones)* Our cousin will not eat you. *(KATE smiles at her gratefully. Exit HELEN L., closing door. WIND begins to blow slightly and distant THUNDER is heard. KATE, left alone, shows her extreme tension by crossing to window L., looks out, hurried look in mirror, glances at door R., then as though in sudden panic goes to door L. DOOR HANDLE R. moves, making noise. KATE faces it, holding herself together; crosses to C. Enter TOM R. KATE registers disgust and disappointment. He looks around, laughs, puzzled.)*

*(WARN Curtain.)*

TOM. *(R.)* Where's your Yankee?

KATE. *(C.)* What have you done with him?

TOM. I thought he must have let himself in. Wilkins says there was no knock.

*(WARN Clock.)*

KATE. She did not hear it for the rain. He's on the doorstep!

TOM. Gad, then he must be fetched to you quickly, or this rain will cool him off. *(Exit TOM R., laughing, leaving door slightly ajar. KATE crosses to chair R. and picks up paper left by TOM; crosses to table C.; puts paper on it. THUNDER increases. She crosses to window up R. and closes it. THUNDER and WIND decrease. Turns quickly as TOM enters R. again, closing door after him.)* Damned if I can find him!

KATE. *(Exasperated)* We saw him, at the door!
                    *(SHADOW Lamp On.)*

TOM. I looked—there was no one there.

KATE. *(Crosses down* R.C., L. *of* TOM*)* Then
*someone* has let him in!

TOM. *(Thinks a moment; laughs)* He's gone
round to the servants' door. Knows his place. *(As
he walks rapidly* L. *and goes out chuckling)* I'll bring
him up the back stairs!

(KATE'S *nervousness increases. Noise of WIND
and RAIN, which has been slightly audible since
HELEN left KATE alone, rises to greater inten-
sity. KATE, with quick, nervous glances about
her, stands* C., *then walks slowly to settee, sits
on it, arranging her dress and folding her hands
in attractive pose. CLOCK strikes without,
twice. Door* R. *commences to open slowly.
KATE sees door, jumps up and walks* R.C., *just
beyond table. It then opens more rapidly, and
as the shadow of a man is thrown upon the wall*
L., *KATE curtseys slowly. As she starts to curtsey the lights commence to dim and the CUR-
TAIN starts coming down slowly. Just as she
has reached the floor the CURTAIN is down.)*

### SLOW CURTAIN

# SCENE II

Scene: *The same room, at the same time, on the same day, in 1928. Most of the furniture remains, but the tone of time has settled upon it, and there are some changes. The windows now have curtains and different shaped pelmets of flowered linen. The curtains are open and the windows shut. A copy of a Georgian pattern on a blue ground, and between them, in place of the tapestry, is a three-quarter length portrait of a young man in eighteenth-century costume, by Sir Joshua Reynolds. Through the windows are bare trees of the Square, seen in pale, rain-washed sunlight. A plain panel replaces the landscape above the fire. The writing-bureau is open, littered with papers and books, and has a lamp on it and an Egyptian antique, a Crux Ansata in blue faience, about four inches high, mounted on small ebony block. No candles on candle-slides. The low tea-table, which before stood folded between window and fireplace, now stands in place of the walnut cabriole-leg table at the L.C. of the stage; it is open; holds another litter of pipes, papers, books, matches and a brass candlestick. To R. of table, an over-stuffed armchair. To L. of table an over-stuffed couch, both covered with the same material as the curtains. Back of the couch stands the old cabriole-leg table (now hidden), and on this a large electric lamp. The console table remains where it was, but it is now bare.*

*As the CURTAIN rises the CLOCK on the landing strikes five, a wheezy, feeble chime, distinct from the full-throated stroke of the clock in the previous scene. And there is a slight NOISE of RAIN.*

MRS. BARWICK, *an elderly housekeeper, dressed in grey with a white apron, opens door R. and stands aside to admit the AMBASSADOR. The AMBASSADOR is elderly, distinguished, suave, urbane, sensitive; crosses to R.C.*

MRS. BARWICK. *(With exaggerated deference, as* AMBASSADOR *walks C.)* If you'll wait here, Your Excellency, I'll tell Mr. Standish. I'm not sure he's dressed, sir. *(Turns on lights. Switch is above door R., which turns on lamps on table rear of settee and on desk, and pin spot on picture up C.)*

AMBASSADOR. *(Turning)* Isn't he well?

MRS. BARWICK. *(Doubtfully)* Oh, yes, sir. I think so, sir. *(She turns to go R.)*

AMBASSADOR. *(Takes step toward her, flattering her a bit)* One moment. Miss Frant has been telling me how you take such good care of Mr. Standish.

MRS. BARWICK. *(Step or two L. She is now R.C. Flattered)* I do my best for him, sir.

AMBASSADOR. Just between ourselves, Miss Frant's a little worried about him.

MRS. BARWICK. *(With a little hesitation)* He's a bit of a quiet one, Your Excellency. I'm sure I hope there's nothing to worry about, begging your pardon, sir. I mean he's a gentleman of moods. Yes, sir, a gentleman of moods.

AMBASSADOR. *(Smiling)* You mean he has good moods—and bad ones?

MRS. BARWICK. Oh, no, sir, I didn't mean it that way. But there are times when he does seem, well, just a bit jumpy.

AMBASSADOR. Really?

MRS. BARWICK. *(Gossiping)* Oh, nothing you could put your finger on, Your Excellency. But it does seem a pity he should stay around the house so much.

AMBASSADOR. Well, it's quite true that I haven't seen him about at all lately, come to think of it. *(Wanders to* C., *looking over room)* Tell me, how does he spend his time cooped up here?

MRS. BARWICK. Well, sir, he seems to me to spend most of his time reading. When he isn't just walking about. *(He faces her.)* I keep hearing him in the night, sir. It seems he's found some old books and papers in the house here. Of course, sir, I don't exactly know, but I sometimes think——

*(Enter* PETER STANDISH R. *He is twenty-six. He is wearing a long, black dressing-gown. Nervous and sensitive. Needs his hair cut. His manner jumpy and feverish.* MRS. BARWICK *is standing above the door at* R.C. *As* PETER *passes her she moves up stage* C. *and closes the curtains on windows* L. *and then* R.)

PETER. Mr. Ambassador! I heard the bell, but I didn't expect such an honor. *(He is coming over to shake hands; stops; hesitates)* Excuse me. I'll just run and put my coat on. *(Is turning away.)*

*(RAIN Dies Out.)*

AMBASSADOR. Nonsense, Mr. Standish. Don't do that. *(They shake hands* R.C.) It's a very becoming dressing-gown.

PETER. But I can't receive an Ambassador like this. I ought to be wearing something—well—more respectful.

AMBASSADOR. Don't worry. The Foreign Secretary once received me in pyjamas.

PETER. Did he? Well, I'll go put mine on if that would seem more appropriate. *(Walking behind set-*

*tee)* I'm not up on how to receive Ambassadors. I don't know that one ever called on me before, but I can manage to give you some tea if you like.

AMBASSADOR. *(Laughs, crosses and sits on settee L.)* How quickly we Yankees take to that, over here.

PETER. Tea, please, Mrs. Barwick. (MRS. BAR-WICK *has come down* R.C., *timing it so she is just at door for* PETER's *line. She goes out* R. PETER *walks about nervously)* Yes, it doesn't take long to get to like tea, does it? I don't mean the tea itself, but what it stands for, that we don't get at home—sort of charming rest period, general let-up and all that sort of thing. *(Moving up* R.C.*)*

AMBASSADOR. But they tell me that even here those dreadful cocktails will soon have sent tea packing from the drawing-room.

PETER. *(Turning back to* AMBASSADOR*)* Yes, cocktails, jazz and one universal traffic block—London's just like New York. *(Lights cigarette from case in pocket of dressing-gown.)*

AMBASSADOR. *(Brushes off cuffs of trousers)* Excepting the weather, which is infinitely worse.

PETER. Has it been bad? I hardly realize there's been any weather.

AMBASSADOR. Haven't been going out much, eh? *(Sitting back in settee.)*

PETER. Not a great deal, no. *(Comes to table* L.C.; *puts match down.)*

AMBASSADOR. You're feeling fit, aren't you, Standish?

PETER. *(As a matter of course, crossing away)* Oh, pretty much as usual. *(Stops suddenly, thinking, turns, looks at* AMBASSADOR*)* What makes you ask?

AMBASSADOR. *(Being chatty)* Nothing in particular. I just wondered why I haven't seen you anywhere all these weeks.

PETER. *(Has come down* R.C.; *turns, facing up)* Well, this house has really been taking all my time.

AMBASSADOR. *(Not looking at him)* Yes, indeed, it is a delightful place. I read about it in "The Times." *(PETER has moved up R.C.; pauses before portrait, looking up at it)* You're really going to settle down here?

PETER. *(Back to audience)* I wouldn't live anywhere else in the world.

AMBASSADOR. Well, I don't blame you. I couldn't make out from the article why your remote English cousin left you the place. Your family didn't know him, from what I gather?

PETER. *(Faces front)* No, but old Standish Pettigrew read a paper of mine on architecture and wrote me about this Queen Anne house. That's how we came to meet. It turned out a Standish ancestor of mine had built the place.

AMBASSADOR. The first Standish who went to America?

PETER. Yes—*(Turns)*—about 1730. *(Stops R. of portrait. PETER is on a level with the AMBASSADOR. PETER points to portrait)* His grandfather.

AMBASSADOR. Hm! *(Rises; looks from portrait to PETER, who is R.C. Then crosses down R.C., looking at PETER and picture; then speaks)* I suppose everybody comments on the likeness? *(Moves to R. of PETER)* You might have sat for it yourself.

PETER. *(Constrained)* Oh, yes; curious, isn't it? His name happens to have been Peter Standish, too.

AMBASSADOR. And that's still more curious. *(Looking up at picture and then at PETER)* Perhaps what impressed your cousin was the coincidence—the likeness, and then the name. *(PETER, about to speak, checks himself. MRS. BARWICK enters R. to table with tea-tray; arranges tea. AMBASSADOR crosses toward desk R., looking things over)* And the house itself is as strange as the legacy—two hundred years old, and yet apparently just as it was, furniture, everything!

PETER. Yes, old Mr. Pettigrew left nearly every stick as he found it.

AMBASSADOR. *(Picks up Crux Ansata from desk; change of tone of voice)* But what about this thing? *(Steps toward* PETER*)* Surely this is Egyptian!

PETER. It's the Crux Ansata, the symbol of life.

AMBASSADOR. Yes, but the symbol of Isis, not of Queen Anne. What's it doing here? *(Hands it to* PETER.*)*

PETER. I don't know. It came with the house. *(*PETER *puts Crux Ansata on table up* C.*)*

AMBASSADOR. *(Turns to tea-table and sees tea set; says as he comes to settee)* Wedgwood! That came with the house, too?

PETER. *(Crosses down to rear of table)* Everything did. *(*MRS. BARWICK *walks* R.*)* Even Mrs. Barwick there. *(Coming down by armchair* R. *of tea-table.* MRS. BARWICK *smiles on them as she goes out* R. PETER *comes down behind tea-table.* AMBASSADOR *sits on* R. *of settee.)* Milk and sugar?

AMBASSADOR. Both, please. *(*PETER, *after pouring tea and handing cup, pours out cup for himself; does not take it; instead, lights cigarette from case, puffs nervously.* AMBASSADOR *sips tea; eats muffin. Conversation continues through this business)* I suppose you'll entertain here a good deal?

PETER. I couldn't afford to.

AMBASSADOR. But when you're married——

PETER. Oh, then! *(As if remembering suddenly; it had not entered his head before)* You'll have to ask Marjorie that.

AMBASSADOR. Charming girl! How lucky for you that she wants to live over here.

PETER. *(Hands him cup of tea)* Oh, she loves the house, too. We're going to do it over.

AMBASSADOR. Do it over? Well, *you* can be trusted not to spoil it.

PETER. There's a new roof needed, and things

like that. *(Turning, crosses up* L. *a step or two)*
That'll all be her doing. You know I've no money.
*(Crosses toward upper* R.*)*

AMBASSADOR. Marjorie was worried, I thought,
that you didn't come to the Embassy reception last
night. *(As he drinks his tea)* She came—*(Glances
at him)*—alone.

PETER. *(Stops now* R. *up stage; looks at* AMBAS-
SADOR*)* Did she? I told her I—didn't feel up to it.

AMBASSADOR. But I thought you said—— H'm.
*(Looks at* PETER, *who is lost in his own thoughts by
now)* It's too bad she's off to America tomorrow.
*(Puts his cup on table.)*

PETER. *(Crosses down* C.*)* She's coming right
back; it's just some family affair; the wedding isn't
postponed. *(He thinks this needs explanation)* I
mean, our plans aren't changed.

AMBASSADOR. *(Facing front)* So she told me.
We had quite a talk.

PETER. *(Sits in armchair; looks at* AMBASSADOR;
*politely challenging)* Yes?

AMBASSADOR. *(After pause, speaks with a slight
personal tone)* And I may as well admit I didn't
come here, Standish, only to see the house.

PETER. *(Dryly)* I *had* flattered myself that what
you really came to see was *me.*

AMBASSADOR. And of course you must think me
a meddling old busybody.

PETER. *(Speaks as soon as he says "meddling")*
Oh, please, Mr. Ambassador! I do appreciate your
kindness. But, you see, there's nothing wrong with
me at all!

AMBASSADOR. Who said there was anything
wrong? I suppose what you meant just now was that
I'd come in to—look you over. Nobody likes being
looked over, when there's no need for it.

PETER. *(Smiling)* Still less, when there is, I suppose.

AMBASSADOR. Anyway, you won't mind my suggesting that London is a very fascinating place.

PETER. *(Enthusiastically, looking over room)* The most fascinating place in the world!

AMBASSADOR. Ah, good! Everybody's talking about the legacy; everybody'd be delighted to meet you. One thing an American Ambassador can do in London is open doors—and such interesting doors, Standish.

PETER. *(Ill at ease; rises; goes over to bureau; speaks as he moves)* I see what you're getting at. It's very thoughtful of you, but I'm very busy just now. Going through some old papers. *(Fumbles with papers on desk.)*

AMBASSADOR. *(Not looking at him)* Too many old papers, Standish. People get morbid and musty when they shut themselves up in old houses. *(Slight pause—they look at each other.)* Marjorie is really quite disturbed about you.

PETER. I wish she wouldn't be. I can't go out just now. *(Turns to desk again)* I've most important work to do here.

AMBASSADOR. The eighteenth century is fascinating, no doubt, but surely your studies are not so pressing——

PETER. *(Without turning, raising voice)* But I've just got to stay here in the house.

AMBASSADOR. *(Perplexed)* Well, I mustn't bore you with questions.

PETER. *(Realizing his rudeness)* Oh, I'm so sorry!

AMBASSADOR. But you *are* making your friends a bit uneasy. Of course—*(Tries to make* PETER *confide in him)*—if there were anything I could do—though if you *will* make a hermit of yourself there probably isn't——

PETER. *(Walks down* L.C.*)* Well, as a matter of fact—— *(Stops, facing* AMBASSADOR.*)*

AMBASSADOR. *(Encouragingly)* Yes?

PETER. *(Nervous excitement)* Well, if you could possibly manage to drop in here two or three times a week, regularly, while Marjorie is gone, I'd appreciate it enormously. *(He sees the look of surprise on* AMBASSADOR'S *face)* Oh, but now I've said it I realize that for *me* to ask such a thing of *you* would be impertinent. And you probably haven't the time, anyway.

AMBASSADOR. *(Puzzled)* But why shouldn't *you* come and see *me?* And make it as often as you like.

PETER. *(Struggling to avoid saying too much)* Thanks, but, well, I don't know if I could.

AMBASSADOR. *(Surprised; says, half to himself)* But surely——

PETER. I mean, I might not want to.

AMBASSADOR. *(Really shocked)* What!

PETER. *(Crosses to him)* Oh, I simply can't make it any clearer just now. *(Sits in armchair.)*

AMBASSADOR. *(All friendliness)* Look here, Standish. Don't you think you ought to get away for a bit?                                    *(WARN Clock.)*

PETER. *(A little wildly; gradually faces him)* Ah! Get away! It would be great to get away, really away, into the blue, wouldn't it? You think I'm a bookworm, don't you? But there still are adventures, inconceivable adventures——

AMBASSADOR. *(After pause; leans over and puts hand on* PETER'S *arm which is on table between them)* Won't you tell *me* what's the trouble?

PETER. I'd like to—it *isn't* trouble—it's—it's wonderful! *(Rises and crosses* L. *in front of settee; turns to him)* Oh, I'd like there to be someone here who *knows*—but I *can't.* We can't talk without using words, so what's the use of talking when there are no words? I understood it all till just now, when you asked me about it, and *now* I don't understand anything about it at all. *(Sits beside him on* L. *of settee)*

Now look here. Here's an idea. Suppose you are in a boat, sailing down a winding stream. You watch the banks as they pass you. You went by a grove of maple trees, up-stream. But you can't see them now, so you saw them in the *past,* didn't you? You're watching a field of clover now; it's before your eyes at this moment, in the *present.* But you don't know yet what's around the bend in the stream there ahead of you. There may be wonderful things, but you can't see them until you get around the bend in the *future,* can you? (AMBASSADOR *nods; he listens politely, betraying no appreciation of anything abnormal in* PETER.) Now remember, *you're* in the boat. But *I'm* up in the sky above you, in a plane. I'm looking down on it all. I can see *all at once!* So the past, present, and future to the man in the boat are all *one* to the man in the plane. Doesn't that show how all Time must really be one? Real Time—real Time is nothing but an idea in the mind of God!

AMBASSADOR. *(In deep thought)* That seems sound metaphysics, but—— *(CLOCK without strikes once.* AMBASSADOR *rises, goes* R., *takes out and consults watch)* I suppose that old grandfather clock came with the house, too? *(Looking* R. *in direction of gong.)*

PETER. Yes, it's ticked away five generations—and it's ticking away now, back in that other time!

AMBASSADOR. *(Turns slowly to* PETER*)* H'm. Other time. *(Looks slowly at picture, then a quick glance at* PETER, *and turns to picture again. Crosses quickly up stage to picture. Looks at* PETER *with a smothered "My God!"* PETER, *"hearing" the silence, looks up at the* AMBASSADOR, *who quickly recovers and speaks in a slightly lighter tone)* A quarter past five already. Wasn't Marjorie coming to tea?

PETER. *(Reassured by the* AMBASSADOR'S *tone,*

*turns front)* Oh, yes, I think she was. She told you? *(Lowers head.)*

AMBASSADOR. *(R. rear. Warily, watching* PETER*)* That portrait now. *(*PETER'S *head comes up.)* One might almost think that—— *(*PETER *looks excitedly at the* AMBASSADOR, *who, hoping he is reaching the cause of* PETER'S *trouble, continues as he crosses down* R.C.*)* Of course, none of us believes in ghosts at home, but over here, in these old houses——

PETER. *(Interrupting)* Who said anything about ghosts? *(Gesture to portrait. Jumps up) He* isn't a ghost. He's alive, alive, alive! I don't mean now; he's dead now, of course; I mean then. *(Crosses to* AMBASSADOR*)* I mean back there in his own time, back there where that clock's ticking, just as it's ticking here, now. *(Hurries excitedly to window* L., *throwing back curtains.* AMBASSADOR *remains* R. *front, watching him.)* How would you like to walk the quiet streets of London in the eighteenth century? And breathe pure air, instead of gasoline! And ride in sedan-chairs, instead of taxicabs? *(Coming down to* AMBASSADOR*)* See Sheridan at the first night of "The School for Scandal" or hear Dr. Johnson say the things Boswell wrote—*(Turning, glances at portrait)*—or watch Reynolds at work on—— *(Turns again and stops, meeting* AMBASSADOR'S *grave, steady look.)*

AMBASSADOR. Yes, Standish, it does sound attractive, but it isn't a thing we'd really do, even if we could. And if we felt anything like *that* coming on, we'd clear out—*(Pats* PETER'S *arm; then crosses a step down* R.*)*—even out of a wonderful house like this.

PETER. *(Walks* L. *in rear of settee as he says, explosively—with the pleasure of anticipation)* Oh, I'd like to see anybody try to clear me out, *now!*

AMBASSADOR. *(Crosses a bit to* C.*)* If we *could*

get back, we'd seem worse than ghosts to all the
people in the other time; we'd seem to them things
that hadn't even been born yet!

PETER. *(At* L. *end of settee)* They wouldn't
know.

AMBASSADOR. *(Crosses to settee and sits)* They'd
find us out, Standish—we'd make *slips.*

PETER. Oh, no, we wouldn't, we couldn't, don't
you see, because what happened back there is real,
does really happen, of course, it *has* happened.
*(*PETER *crosses in front of settee to* C., *looking up
at picture as he speaks)* So if anybody *could* change
places with somebody back there, it would only be a
charade; he'd have to do all the things that the other
fellow had done. *(Turns to* AMBASSADOR*)* He
couldn't change anything in the eighteenth century
that really *had happened* in the eighteenth century,
could he?

AMBASSADOR. H'm. Change places.

PETER. *(Excitedly)* Yes, *change places!* *(*AM-
BASSADOR *rises.)* Oh, but I was a fool to tell you.
And now I suppose you'll go and call up a specialist.
*(Crosses toward desk Right.)*

AMBASSADOR. *(Makes motion of "Of course not"
—entertains idea of changing places)* I still don't
see what credentials we could take back into the
past that would make them accept us as even human.

PETER. *(Triumphantly)* Ah, credentials! *(Rummages among papers; comes back waving small book
above his head)* Here's my passport!

AMBASSADOR. What's that? *(*AMBASSADOR *and*
PETER *sit on settee—*PETER R. *of him.)*

PETER. *(Waves book toward portrait)* It's *his*
diary! *(Sits by him on settee, opening leaves; speaks
with feverish rapidity. During this* AMBASSADOR
*watches not the diary, which* PETER *is showing him,
but* PETER'S *face)* He's put everything down! I've
learned it almost word for word. That's what I've

been doing! *(Looks in diary)* His trip from New
York took twenty-seven days, in a barque called the
*General Wolfe*. No wonder he calls the trip "dreary."
He fought under Washington. The war was just
over, but he made friends with an English Major
Clinton on the boat. Peter was an inventor, when
all that was just beginning, that's why he wants to
see into our wonderful new age of machinery that
he senses ahead of him. *(Turning leaves)* It says
Reynolds wouldn't finish the portrait. *(Turns to picture)* But he did finish it. It's obviously all Reynolds'! Look! *(Points to passages)* He married the
elder sister, you see! Kate—that's Kate Pettigrew.
They lived in this house. I've other papers about
them—they had children, who died here. See! There
was a younger sister, Helen. Her people tried to
force her into a marriage she hated. The diary stops
before that was settled. Look! There's even something about a Kashmir shawl that Helen's aunt in
the country gave her just before Peter came over.
Minute details about everything, you see! *(Drops
diary beside* AMBASSADOR *on settee)* And I've got
his letters, courting Kate before he'd ever seen her.
*(Dashes to desk; sits; rummages)* They were in a
secret drawer here. I've got the letter Peter wrote
Lady Anne—the girl's mother—when he'd just arrived from New York. *(Jumps up)* Oh, damn! I
know where I left it! You *must* see that! (PETER
*hurries out* L.)

(AMBASSADOR *looks after him intently, then picks
up diary, looks at it, then at picture. Rises and
crosses slowly to picture. He is standing up* C.,
*back to audience; puts hands behind his back,
holding diary in his hands.* MRS. BARWICK *opens
door* R. MARJORIE FRANT *enters. An attractive
girl in the late twenties, dressed with sensible
good taste.* MRS. BARWICK *goes out.)*

"Berkeley Square"

Act II, See Page 70

MARJORIE. *(Stops just inside door)* Hello, Mr. Ambassador! *(He turns. She takes a step toward him)* What a surprise! Isn't Peter here?

AMBASSADOR. *(They shake hands, R. rear)* He'll be back in a minute, Marjorie.

MARJORIE. *(Takes off hat; puts it on table L.; walks to settee as she says)* I suppose you came because of what I said last night, and I'm so grateful for your sympathy and your——

AMBASSADOR. *(Follows her. Interrupts; speaks gravely and quickly; puts diary on table between settee and armchair)* I'm going to leave you together.

MARJORIE. *(Slight pause. Alarmed at his tone— sits on settee)* Why, what's the matter?

AMBASSADOR. If you have to sail tomorrow, try your very best to persuade him to go with you. But whatever happens, he must be got out of this house!

MARJORIE. But why——

AMBASSADOR. When you leave him come to me at the Embassy.

MARJORIE. Yes, but——

AMBASSADOR. There's no time now to explain. Sh! *(Turns; moves to R.)*

PETER. *(Enters L., reading letter; comes to AMBASSADOR R.C. down stage. PETER'S back to MARJORIE)* Here it is. Read it. *(He puts the letter into the AMBASSADOR'S hand.)*

AMBASSADOR. *(Reading)* "From the Blue Boar in Jermyn Street, October 23rd, 1784."

PETER. *(Triumphantly)* October 23rd! That's today!

AMBASSADOR. *(Looks up, then reads, half to himself)* "October 23rd, 1784. Honored Madam: Having arrived within the hour, traveling by post from Plymouth, I make haste to dispatch you this intimation that I shall do myself the honor to wait upon yourself, my fair cousins, and Mr. Pettigrew, at a half after five this evening, in Berkley Square."

(PETER *looks at wrist watch.*) "I subscribe myself, Madam, your most obedient cousin and humble servant, Peter Standish. To the Lady Anne Pettigrew." *(He hands the letter back to* PETER.)

PETER. The paper's yellow, and the ink faded— and yet Lady Anne is just reading that letter, *now!*

MARJORIE. *(Who has risen)* Peter!

PETER. *(Starts, turns and faces* MARJORIE*)* How long have you been here?

MARJORIE. Only a minute.

PETER. *(Warmly)* Oh—I do hope you have a nice crossing—you're sailing tomorrow—isn't it? (MARJORIE'S *lips tremble—looks away from* PETER. AMBASSADOR *intervenes, lifting scene.*)

AMBASSADOR. *(Looking at watch)* You've made me forget an appointment, Standish. Goodbye, Marjorie. *(To* PETER, *as* PETER *follows him to door* R.*)* No, don't come down. *(Meaningly)* I'll drop in here, Peter, as you suggested.

PETER. Oh, thank you! *(They shake hands. Exit* AMBASSADOR, *leaving door ajar.*)

MARJORIE. *(Not a reproach)* Peter, what made you speak to me that way?

PETER. *(Turns; walks to her before armchair)* Was I rude? Forgive me. *(Kisses her)* I was thinking of something else.

MARJORIE. What?

PETER. *(Crosses up to desk; handles papers)* Only a job I've got to do. *(Lights cigarette from case.)*

MARJORIE. What were you talking about?

PETER. Just some eighteenth-century people.

MARJORIE. *(Sits on* R. *of settee)* You're so nervous! Smoking too much, dear. (PETER *crushes out cigarette on desk.*) Only a month now till I'll be living here to look after you. And you need it, Peter!

PETER. *(Walking across to armchair)* You don't want to marry me, Marjorie dear. You want only to look after me.

MARJORIE. One goes with the other, doesn't it?

PETER. You're so patient with me, so good, so kind. *(He sits.)*

MARJORIE. Peter, I want you to do something specially nice for me. I don't want to leave you. I want to be with you. Pack up and sail with me to-morrow—we'll come right back.

PETER. *(Startled, almost shrinking from her)* Oh, no, I can't. *(Lamely)* I'd rather be here.

MARJORIE. *(Hurt)* Rather be here than with me? *(Speaks with forced lightness)* You do care more for this old house than—— *(She hesitates a moment —then speaks sincerely)* If you love me you will come!

PETER. I can't!

MARJORIE. *(Rises)* You won't, you mean. *(Rises, crosses to down L., turns and faces him)* Peter, darling, I don't know what's the matter, but you're not well; you're not yourself. Well—*(Walks to front of settee)*—if you won't come, then I won't go. I'm going to stay in London. *(Sits on settee.)*

*(WARN Wind.)*

PETER. *(Distressed; rises)* You told me you *had* to go!

MARJORIE. You want to get rid of me! You're so strange, you hold me off from you!

PETER. *(Sits beside her on settee)* Marjorie, listen. I must have this month here alone. Trust me. *(They are L.C.)*          *(WARN Black Out.)*

MARJORIE. But, Peter, dear—you're so strange, you've never been like this. Why won't you tell me what it is? I *will* trust you, if you'll just tell me—

PETER. *(Distressed. Turns from her; moves C.)* But I can't. You'd—— No, no—you mustn't ask it—— *(Stops; listens. NOISE of coach. In a low, tense whisper)* What's that? *(He crosses rapidly to window R. and holds back curtains.)*

MARJORIE. What's what? *(Faint NOISE of WIND and RAIN.)*

PETER. *(Turns at window)* Sounded like a wagon rattling over cobblestones. It seemed to stop here. *(Crosses a step down* C.; *looks at his watch)* But there's only your car at the door. *(Crosses again to window—looks out—then crosses to* R. *of and below picture, looking at it.)*      *(WARN Shadow Lamp.)*

MARJORIE. *(Still standing before settee)* I didn't hear anything. Cobblestones, in Berkley Square? Why, they've had wood blocks for ages; it's quieter even than our asphalt in New York. Peter, what's the matter with you? *(The electric LIGHTS go out. NOISE of WIND and THUNDER. RAIN increases until* PETER'S *exit.)* Oh, dear! *(Sits on settee.)*      *(BLACK Out.)*

PETER. I'll light a candle. *(Lights candle on tea-table.)*

*(LIGHTS Up.)*

MARJORIE. *(Sitting on settee)* Darling, your hand's shaking! Ring, Peter. Get somebody to fix the lights!

*(Enter* MRS. BARWICK R., *carrying candle. She stops a few steps inside door.* PETER *faces her behind tea-table, holding candle.)*

MRS. BARWICK. A gentleman to see you, sir. Just as he came in the lights went out all over the house. He's all muffled up.

*(WARN Curtain.)*

MARJORIE. Who is he?

MRS. BARWICK. When I asked his name he only said again, "Mr. Peter Standish." I've shown him into the study. *(*PETER *looks quickly at picture.* PETER *walks slowly to door* R. *as if in a trance, crossing* MRS. BARWICK.)*

*(WARN Clock.)*

MARJORIE. Peter, who is it? *(He walks on, unheeding.)* Peter! It's my very last evening. *(He hesitates at door, without facing her, as though he was going to speak—thinks better of it and continues on out the door, closing it behind him. The THUNDER and WIND builds to a ROAR as he goes out and stops DEAD when door has been closed five seconds. Silence for count of five, then WIND, RAIN and THUNDER pick up softly.* MARJORIE *moves* C. *Hysterical)* Who is this man?

MRS. BARWICK. I don't know, Miss.

*(SHADOW Lamp On.)*

MARJORIE. *(Crying)* He heard noises in the street when there were no noises. *(WARN Black Out.)*

MRS. BARWICK. Here, Miss, take this. (MRS. BARWICK *hands* MARJORIE *candle; crosses as she speaks)* He's not himself, Miss. I'll get a lamp and then see to the lights. *(She goes out L.)*

*(Door R. opens slowly. Pale light from candle carried by the man who is opening the door. WIND and RAIN heard more loudly again until CURTAIN. CLOCK on landing strikes twice.* MARJORIE *runs to door with a cry of recognition.)*

MARJORIE. Peter! (MARJORIE *stops suddenly, face to face with man at door, who is invisible to audience. Steps back)* Peter! I'm afraid of you! *(Little nervous laugh)* Isn't it absurd, to be afraid of my Peter! *(Another step back.)*

## QUICK CURTAIN

*(Curtain halfway down. BLACK OUT.* MARJORIE *screams and puts out candle by hitting it on top with palm of her hand as she screams.)*

## CURTAIN

# SCENE III

SCENE: *The room in 1784. CLOCK is heard to strike twice, an instant before the CURTAIN goes up. The CURTAIN rises at the exact moment when it fell upon Scene I. NOISE of RAIN. The footlights fade in as CURTAIN rises. Curtains on window closed and windows closed.*

KATE *discovered at* c., *just going to curtsey. Noise of WIND and RAIN STOPS, as* PETER *enters slowly, in the costume of the man in the portrait. Dazed, he stares at her, shrinking back against the door, his hand on the knob. Staring at him, she curtseys, saying:*

KATE. Your servant, sir. *(Pause)* At your service, cousin.

PETER. *(At length)* Who—are you?

KATE. Kate Pettigrew.

PETER. *(In awe and wonder)* Kate—Pettigrew!

(KATE *walks toward him; extends her hand to be kissed.* PETER *takes step forward doubtfully, as though not quite sure whether* KATE *is really flesh and blood. At length he takes her hand, awkwardly, bows and kisses it, then retreats two steps toward door.)*

KATE. I bid you welcome, on Mother's behalf.

PETER. Your mother. The Lady Anne. I trust she is well?

38

KATE. Indeed yes, I thank you. *(Awkward silence.)*

PETER. It's raining awfully hard.

*(RAIN Dies Out.)*

KATE. *(Still extremely nervous)* Yes, the weather has been wretched. But you'll find it nearly always so in London.

PETER. You have a great many fogs, haven't you?

KATE. Indeed, yes, there was one last week that lasted three days. And they're getting worse than they used to be, with people burning more sea coal.

PETER. *(At length, to cover his own lack of resource)* You seem a little embarrassed, cousin.

KATE. *(With nervous laugh)* You are not exactly at your ease yourself.

PETER. You've never seen me before, have you?

KATE. That seems a strange question.

PETER. I mean, am I—different from what you expected?

KATE. Indeed, I think you are, cousin. We were led to look for a bold, forward fellow.

PETER. I'm a little surprised, too—I thought that Kate would be—well——

KATE. *(With a touch of spirit)* Not so timid? I trust you will find me not always such a ninny, and my conversation not limited to the weather. But I'm sure you've had a tiring journey after your voyage. Come, sit down and tell me about it. (KATE *sits on* R. *of settee.* PETER *takes step toward her; remains standing* R.C.) You said nothing of your voyage in your letter.

PETER. My letter!

KATE. *(Surprised)* To my mother, from the "Blue Boar," where I hope they have made you comfortable.

PETER. My letter from the "Blue Boar"! *(Looking to her for confirmation)* Of course. I went there when the coach came in, and I've just come over from America.

KATE. *(Surprised—teasing him)* We did not think you had come from Poland. *(Smiles.)*

PETER. In the *General Wolfe*.

KATE. *(Teasing)* Really! In the packet? Did you not swim across? *(Laughs.)*

PETER. *(Now reassured, laughs with her)* In the *General Wolfe*—it took twenty-seven dreary days.

KATE. I suppose the sea is always dreary, but you had a swift passage.

PETER. *(After pause)* Yes, the wind was with us all the way; we must have almost beat the record.

KATE. Record? *(She looks at him, puzzled.)*

PETER. *(Realizing his mistake)* Oh, that's an American word. I'm afraid you'll find that I use a lot of strange phrases. We're developing a new language over there.

KATE. You must instruct me in it.

PETER. *(Goes to settee, sits by her awkwardly, still a little afraid)* Kate, forgive me for being such a boor.

KATE. *(Nervous, but coquettish since she likes him)* Your manners have been unexceptionable.

PETER. But hardly appropriate for a man who has just met his betrothed for the first time.

KATE. Are we betrothed? I had not heard of it.

PETER. Come, don't tease me. It's been practically all arranged in our letters. *(Puts his hand on hers. She faces him; he clumsily steals a kiss. They both rise.)*

KATE. *(Rises, shrinking back coquettishly)* There's nothing settled yet, and this is more in keeping with what I have heard of your rough ways at home, sir.

PETER. *(Taking his cue from her coquettish tone, and rather awkwardly attempting to act as he imagines his role demands)* Come, Kate, don't call me

"Sir." I'll certainly not call you Miss. Call me Peter! Say it!

KATE. *(Protestingly)* Sir! Cousin! (PETER *makes to hold her hands. She escapes, laughing, to* L. *and behind settee)* Peter, then! You'll think me a brazen creature to laugh at your clowning, but I'll have no more of it!

PETER. *(In front of settee, facing to* L.; *they talk across it)* Come, Kate, it's all arranged. The settlement was to be fifteen thousand pounds, wasn't it? That's all for the lawyers. We two needed only a kiss to make sure.

KATE. I vow you are the most abrupt man! You are but the audacious fellow I told Helen we must expect.

PETER. Helen? Oh, yes, your sister. (KATE *comes around* L. *corner of settee in front of it,* PETER *standing in front of small table.)*

KATE. You've not even asked Mother's permission to pay your addresses.

PETER. Must I do that?

KATE. *(Looking at him, then on the ground)* Is it not invariably done?

PETER. Er—not in New York.

KATE. *(Chaffing)* This is London. These are strange manners you bring us from the United States. And do visitors in New York walk into people's houses without so much as a by your leave?

PETER. *(Disturbed)* I rang the bell.

KATE. *(Again astonished)* Bell? What bell?

PETER. I mean, the knocker.

KATE. We saw you alight from your coach, but —who let you in?

PETER. The door was ajar. I walked in—to get out of the rain.

KATE. *(Accepting this)* We wondered—— But your clothes are dry! *(Stepping back a pace from him.)*

PETER. I wore a cloak.

KATE. *(Staring at his boots)* Even your boots are
dry! (PETER, *disturbed and at a loss, turns from
her, fumbling for cigarette case in waistcoat pocket.
Absent-mindedly opens and extends silver case to
her.* KATE *walks to him in front of small table.
Looking at case)* I had no miniature of *you*, although
I wrote and asked you for one.

PETER. *(Looks at miniature, astonished; puts it
back in pocket, absent-mindedly fumbling in another
pocket as he remarks)* Well, I preferred to present
myself in the flesh. *(Brings jewelled bracelet out of
other pocket; looks at it.)*

KATE. Oh, what is that? (PETER *gallantly hands
it to* KATE, *saying "For you."*) Most charming. But
—is this not a little premature?

PETER. *(Puzzled)* Premature?

KATE. *(Sits on settee, holding bracelet)* Does not
this signify, in New York, what it does here?

PETER. *(Understanding)* Of course. If you will
have the declaration formal, I know how it was done.
*(Correcting himself)* —how it is done. *(Goes on
one knee before her)* Miss Pettigrew, fair cousin,
will you be my wife?

KATE. *(Laughing)* You go much too fast.

PETER. *(He has seized both her hands)* You'll
not dislike me for that.

KATE. I've not said that I mislike you! *(She lets
him slip the bracelet over her wrist.* LADY ANNE
*enters* L. PETER *springs up and back in alarm and
confusion.* KATE *also rises, remains standing in
front and to* L. *of settee.* HELEN *enters, crosses to*
C., *followed by* THROSTLE.) Ma'am, I present our
cousin, Mr. Peter Standish. (PETER *stares at her,
standing* R.C. *down stage.* LADY ANNE *curtseys,* L.C.
*They both advance, and he kisses her hand,* C.)

LADY ANNE. *(Curtseys. Gushing)* Welcome, ten
thousand welcomes, dear, dear cousin.

PETER. Lady Anne, forgive me. Kate's beauties have quite deprived me of my wits and speech.

KATE. A deceiving tongue you've brought with you from New York—Peter. (LADY ANNE *looks from one to the other. After sigh of satisfaction, walks to settee; sits* R. HELEN *advances above small table, while* THROSTLE *walks to console table up stage* C. *and remains standing there.*)

LADY ANNE. Can you take your eyes from Kate to spare a nod for your cousin Helen? (PETER *and* HELEN *stare and step toward each other.* KATE *sits in chair extreme* L. *front.* HELEN *curtseys Center.* PETER *advances and kisses her hand there.* TOM *slouches in* L. *and stops behind* HELEN.)

HELEN. Your servant, sir.

PETER. Your servant, cousin.

LADY ANNE. And our dear friend, Mr. Throstle, Mr. Standish. (PETER *steps back* R. THROSTLE *comes down two steps. They bow.*)

PETER. Mr. Throstle, of the Academy of Painters in Water Color?

THROSTLE. I had not supposed a name so insignificant——

PETER. Oh, I have—been reading about you.

LADY ANNE. And your cousin Tom.

TOM. *(On introduction walks up to* PETER, R., *passing between* HELEN *and* THROSTLE. *Sniggers as they bow)* The jest is against me, sir. I had thought to call a tailor in to you before you could face the town.

PETER. *(Surveys his clothes uneasily)* I'm afraid the jest is against me.

TOM. No, 'pon my oath; your coat's a better fit than mine, and your scarf's perfection, sir. Eh, Kate? Eh, Mother? Isn't he in the tone? *(They laugh as* PETER *turns to them.*)

LADY ANNE. This sudden storm, cousin, so unusually violent for the time of year—I hope you were not incommoded.

KATE. His clothes were dry!

PETER. *(Crosses a step to* R.C. TOM *gives stage to* R.*)* Oh, I was already in the coach when it really started to pour—I think it's clearing—— *(Crosses to* R. *window; glances out; exclaims involuntarily)* Oh, four lackeys with a sedan-chair! *(He turns quickly, realizing his mistake. They are all staring at him.)*

HELEN. You speak, sir, as though you'd never before seen a sedan chair.

PETER. *(Crosses down* L.C.*)* I don't believe I'd noticed one.

THROSTLE. *(Pleasantly)* Sir, I passed a dozen but now, and so must have you, on your way hither from the "Blue Boar."

PETER. *(Lightly)* I didn't see them.

LADY ANNE. Are the New York quality not borne abroad in their chairs?

PETER. No—they ride in—coaches.

LADY ANNE. Sit here by Kate, cousin. (PETER *sits by* LADY ANNE *on settee* L. TOM *sits before desk.* THROSTLE *brings up chair from beside console table for* HELEN; *she sits in it, behind and to* R. *of small table.* THROSTLE *walks* R.; *stops near* TOM.*)* Your boxes shall be fetched. Of course you remain with us.

PETER. *(Sits* L. *of* LADY ANNE*)* If you will have me.

LADY ANNE. *If* we will have you! And had you an agreeable voyage, dear cousin?

PETER. A dreary twenty-seven days in the *General Wolfe.*

KATE. My brother has but now met with a shipmate of yours.

PETER. *(Nervous and alert)* Indeed? Who was that?

Tom. Major Clinton.

Peter. Oh, yes, of course, a most agreeable fellow.

Tom. Clinton told me of your ingenious inventions, sir. *(Laughs)* Now that you're rid of us, you seem to think you're going to do great things in the Col—— (Throstle *coughs a warning.*) —the United States.

Peter. Oh, I suppose we are. *(Whimsically)* Our forefathers—I mean we—have brought forth on that continent a new nation, conceived in liberty and dedicated to the proposition that all men are created equal.

Lady Anne. *(Astonished)* All men—created equal!

Peter. That is the proposition.

Throstle. But, sir, that proposition is absurd.

Peter. *(Laughs)* Of course it is absurd! (Throstle *turns to* Tom. *They laugh together at* Peter.)

Kate. I'm fascinated by your strange theories that life in the future is all going to be so changed— and so exciting——

Tom. *(With a faint sneer)* Especially in the United States.

Peter. Exciting? Oh, very, for people who like bustle, and efficiency, but I'm sure people like—ourselves, in a hundred years, would give their eyes to get back here again!

Tom. *(Rises; walks* c.*)* We shall be damnably mouldy in a hundred years. But if the present interests you, sir, I'm your man—Cousin Tom will show you the town!

Peter. *(It bursts out with great pleasure)* Oh, yes!

Tom. Where shall I take him first? Cox's Museum and Ranelagh and Vauxhall——

Peter. *(Eagerly)* I want to see everything!

THROSTLE. *(Comes behind and to* R. *of* HELEN'S *chair, the armchair up* C. *by* R.*)* Should your tastes prove more sober than Mr. Tom's, sir, my poor services as cicerone——

LADY ANNE. Yes, the exhibition at the Royal Academy!

TOM. *(Disgusted)* Gad's life! *(Turns* R. *and leans on door.)*

THROSTLE. Sir, should you care to join me there tomorrow, I should be glad to present you to the President of the Academy, Sir Joshua.

PETER. Reynolds! *(A slight gesture and glance at panel where picture hangs in 1928.* THROSTLE *glances too.* PETER *quickly goes on)* Do you think he would paint my portrait?

TOM. Ay—at a hundred guineas.

PETER. Five hundred dollars—a Reynolds! *(Shakes his head slowly at the thought of the cheapness.* THROSTLE, *looking front, does the same, but thinking of the "large" cost.)*

LADY ANNE. Indeed, a monstrous price! But he's the fashion.

PETER. *(Resumes seat. To* THROSTLE*)* Oh, thank you! Of course I'll come. My curiosity will wear you all out. But I mustn't make myself a nuisance— *(Turns to* KATE, *who is seated chair* L. *below door)* —except to my cousins——

TOM. You may regard our friend Throstle, cousin, as one of the family.

PETER. Indeed?

TOM. I think I may go so far as to say, as a prospective brother-in-law. Eh, Throstle? *(*HELEN *rises in mingled shame and anger.* THROSTLE *turns protestingly to* TOM. *General constraint.* PETER *looks at her, rising abruptly.)*

HELEN. *(Choking back her tears. Smiles sourly at* PETER*)* Poor Tom is always putting his foot in it! *(Turns away, leaning on door, facing out front.)*

PETER. *(Greatly embarrassed, looks quickly at* HELEN, *then* KATE, *and finally, receiving nothing from any of them, he speaks to* LADY ANNE *in some confusion)* I've been admiring your Queen Anne chairs, Lady Anne. (THROSTLE *turns to* TOM; *they register contempt at* PETER'S *breach of taste.)*

LADY ANNE. Queen Anne! Ay, to our shame, it is so the wars have impoverished so many of us here, dear cousin; alas, we cannot afford to rid ourselves of our old rubbish. *(There is an awkward silence.* PETER *resumes seat.)*

KATE. Do you dance, cousin?

PETER. Why, of course.

KATE. *(Pleased)* I could not have endured you else.

TOM. Our cousin has all the talents.

LADY ANNE. Helen's birthday, indeed, comes at a most opportune moment, cousin.

KATE. Yes, there's to be a ball here next week.

PETER. Er—what do you dance, in London?

KATE. Why, what everbody dances. Gavottes, minuets.

PETER. I fear I shall disgrace you. *(He has been looking at* HELEN*)* Your birthday dance, cousin! Then your aunt's gift is your birthday present!

LADY ANNE. Gift! What gift, Helen?

PETER. Why, the Kashmir shawl.

KATE. Oh, Helen, you sly puss!

HELEN. *(Rises. Bewildered, to* PETER*)* Is it a shawl?

LADY ANNE. *(To* HELEN*)* Why, pray, have you kept this from us?

HELEN. Aunt Willoughby gave me a parcel for my birthday, but I wasn't to open it until then. *(Crosses* L. *via rear of settee)* I haven't opened it. I don't know what's in it. (ALL *but* PETER *make some exclamation. There is a pause.* HELEN *goes*

*out quickly* L. TOM *rises; comes down front.*
THROSTLE *moves down and* C.)

TOM. Damme, what conjuror's trick is this?

PETER. *(Embarrassed, worried)* Why all this fuss
about a shawl?

KATE. But how did you know about Helen's present?

LADY ANNE. How do you know it's a shawl?

KATE. *(Wagging finger)* I believe 'tis an American joke.

PETER. *(Puzzled)* Joke? (HELEN *re-enters with
Kashmir shawl; stops* C. *Left of* THROSTLE, *showing it to them all.* THROSTLE *fingers it.*)

TOM. A shawl, so it is, by Gad!

KATE. Cousin, how did you know?

LADY ANNE. Indeed, how, cousin? Come, come,
sir.

PETER. I'm heartily sorry. I got muddled somehow.

TOM. *(Walks* C.) Muddled, sir, muddled! 'Tis
not you who are muddled!

KATE. Have pity on us, you tricksy man.

HELEN. Indeed, cousin, plague us no more.
(PETER *is silent.*)

TOM. 'S life, you make rare sport of us, sir.

THROSTLE. *(Between* HELEN *and* TOM) My
friend, Mr. Boswell, says such feats as this are common in Scotland.

LADY ANNE. Come, we'll take no refusal. How
did you know?

PETER. I've forgotten.

LADY ANNE. How can you be so teasing? Come,
come!

TOM. Here's a rival for you, Helen.

HELEN. I'm sure 'tis very strange.

TOM. Lookee, cousin, can you read thoughts?

PETER. Of course not!

HELEN. *(To* TOM) It wasn't reading thoughts.

*I* didn't know. (*Turns to* PETER. TOM *and* THROSTLE *go together* R.C.)

KATE. Pray solve us your riddle, Peter!

PETER. I must have heard about the shawl. I told you I'd forgotten where. (*Puts head in hands.*)

LADY ANNE. Sir, you but now reached London from America.

HELEN. (*One step toward* PETER *to just in front of small table; then stops, putting shawl down on table* C.) I'm afraid Cousin Peter is not well.

PETER. (*Rises; looks at her gratefully—glad of excuse*) No, I'm not. I can't think. The truth is, I suppose it's the trip. I've rather a tiresome headache. (*Backs up a step to rear of and* L. *of settee.*)

LADY ANNE. (*Rises*) Your poor head. Oh, you must rest, after so long a journey.

PETER. (*Just behind* L. *end of settee*) Yes—a very long journey.

KATE. (*Rises; moves up to* PETER) I'll fetch you a compress. (*Exits* L. TOM *and* THROSTLE *exchange a word,* R. TOM *goes to window* R.; *looks out, as* THROSTLE *comes to* LADY ANNE; *kisses her hand.* LADY ANNE *crosses to doors* L.)

THROSTLE. I must take my leave. (*Crosses to* LADY ANNE, *kissing her hand—then turns and kisses* HELEN's *hand; comes to* R.C., *then turns, bows to* PETER) Command me, sir, if and when Tom's more full-blooded entertainment palls.

PETER. (*Bowing*) Indeed I shall.

TOM. (*At window*) The rain has stopped, Throstle. Come to the stables and see my new smoker from Newmarket. (*Crossing down to door* R., *opens it, then steps above it to allow* THROSTLE *to exit before him.*)

THROSTLE. (*Walking* R.) If you'll come to Duke Street and see my new aquatint——

TOM. (*As they go out* R. *together*) Damn your aquatints!

THROSTLE. *(Tittering)* Damn your horses, then!
*(Exeunt* TOM *and* THROSTLE, R.*)*

LADY ANNE. *(To* PETER*)* I must see to your
room, sir. (PETER *is standing between* HELEN, R.,
*and* LADY ANNE, L. *He walks* L. *and holds door
open for* LADY ANNE. *As she goes out, curtseys)*
We are so, so happy to greet you here, dear, dear
cousin. (PETER *bows, turns and finds himself facing*
HELEN, *who has crossed above settee as though to
go out. They look at one another for a moment.)*

HELEN. Won't you sit down, cousin?

PETER. *(Both above settee—facing each other)*
Thanks so much for helping me out.

HELEN. *(Smiling)* There wasn't anything really
the matter with your head, was there?

PETER. No, not exactly, but you were the only one
who saw—or, at any rate, you made them stop both-
ering me.

HELEN. *(Crosses to below settee to about* L.C.*)*
I didn't see how you could know about my shawl.

PETER. *(Crosses to below settee—standing down
L.)* Please be an angel and don't ask me any more
about the confounded thing.

HELEN. *(Sits on* R. *of settee)* If you wish.

PETER. Oh, thank you. *(Sits settee* L. *of* HELEN*)*
Just as soon as I saw you I felt, "here's someone I
can talk to." You'll help me out here, won't you?
*(Sits beside her.)*

HELEN. How can *I* help you, cousin?

PETER. It's all so strange.

HELEN. Strange?

PETER. All this.

HELEN. England? London?

PETER. Yes. I didn't think it would, but it makes
me—uncomfortable. You see that. I see that you
see it. I—I feel like a fish out of water.

HELEN. *(Turns head away)* Kate will soon put
you at your ease.

PETER. I'm sure she'll try. Oh, there's so much I want to ask you, I don't know where to begin.

HELEN. *(Looks at him)* We're all most anxious to make you feel at home here.

PETER. Helen—are you really engaged to Mr.— Mr.——

HELEN. Mr. Throstle.

PETER. Forgive me. It's none of my business. But I thought your brother said——

HELEN. *(Flashing. Turning from him, facing to R.)* He had no *right* to say it!

PETER. I thought so! I could see that you weren't in love with him.

HELEN. *(Turns back to him)* Do you think that's reason enough not to marry him?

PETER. Of course. Well, Helen, we'll make a bargain. You help me out and I'll back you up.

HELEN. *(Rising, looking down at PETER, and speaking eagerly)* Will you?

PETER. *(Rising)* Yes, I will! But—— *(He hesitates, seeing his difficulty)* I'd forgotten. I can't interfere with things that happen, that really *do* happen. *(Lamely)* My position here is so—so unusual.

HELEN. Oh, but you can. You don't realize yet what your position here is. They'll do anything you wish.

PETER. Yes, but—— Oh, you can't understand this—— Perhaps you really *do* marry him, after all.

HELEN. Never! *(Turning, walks C.)*

*(WARN Chimes.)*

PETER. That's the spirit! I don't like the little fellow. (HELEN *turns to face him. He walks up to her* C.) And, anyway, I'm sure there isn't anybody good enough—— Why do you look at me like that?

HELEN. I don't know.

PETER. *(Earnestly)* Is there anything strange, or wrong, about me?

HELEN. Strange, or wrong?

PETER. I'm an American, you know. Just come into this new world. That's why I'm nervous.

(*WARN Curtain.*)

HELEN. Is it? (*Removes her eyes from* PETER'S *for first time, almost like coming out of a trance*) My sister will join you in a moment. (*Turns to go* R.)

PETER. (*Following her* R. *front. Pleadingly*) Don't go. Just to see you steadied me. I've nothing in common with all the others.

HELEN. (*Turning to him at door. Meaningly*) *All* the others?

PETER. Of course!

HELEN. (*With a smile*) All but Kate. (*Exits* R., *closing door.*)

(PETER *moves quickly as though to open door and follow her; checks himself. He stands a moment, disheartened and afraid; walks* C.; *looks around the room. He goes up to the writing-desk as to an old friend, strokes it, looks at familiar chairs and the carpet. Standing back stage* C., *he pulls out miniature case, opens it again absent-mindedly, snaps it shut in disappointment. Then he opens it again and gazes at the miniature. He looks at the door* L. *through which* KATE *has gone out, then, slowly putting case back in his pocket, at the door* R. *Musing a moment, he turns again, sees himself in the mirror beside the fireplace, touches wig and his collar, passes his hand over his coat. He goes up to the tapestry suspended over console table where the picture hangs in 1928, and as he is gazing at it the* CHIMES *from a neighboring church tower are heard.* PETER *hears them; walks to window* L.; *slowly opens curtains and raises the window. The* CHIMES *are LOUDER.* PETER, *his left hand holding the curtain, his right knee on the window-seat, looks out into Berkley Square for some time, motionless.)*

PETER. *(The thrill of the adventure, and all his appreciation of what he sees, in his voice)* Berkeley Square! I thought it would look like this!

*(The CHIMES continue to play. The CURTAIN falls slowly.)*

## CURTAIN

# ACT TWO

SCENE I: *Late at night. The room is brilliantly lit by the candles. A string orchestra is playing MUSIC in the drawing-room* L., *and the double doors are open. An easel bearing canvas is propped in the corner between the writing-bureau and the rear wall. Some of the furniture has been rearranged. The settee has been pushed back and to the* R.C.; *the tea-table, folded again, stands against* L. *end of settee, and the stool that was before the writing-bureau is placed to* L. *of settee at such an angle that two people sitting on settee and stool respectively appear in profile to audience. The armchair has been placed before the* L. *window and the pair of walnut chairs are downstage* L. *at right angles to each other, as though placed in position by two people who had been talking. The fire stool and the cabriole table have been removed.*

MISS BARRYMORE *and* MAJOR CLINTON, *in uniform, enter* L.

CLINTON. I trust that dancing has given you an appetite, Miss Susan.

MISS BARRYMORE. *(Crosses to* R.C., *followed by* CLINTON) Perhaps a glass of sherry and a biscuit—

CLINTON. There's a very large banquet spread below tonight; indeed, a novelty in *this* house.

MISS BARRYMORE. The cousin from the Colonies will pay. *(Faces him* R.C.) Ah, Major Clinton, *you*

54

can tell us how much money he *really* has. Some
say, twenty-five thousand a year!

CLINTON. *(With a laugh)* I'll wager there can be
no such fortune in the whole of Yankeedoodledom.

MISS BARRYMORE. *(Continues cross to below R.C.)*
Scoff as you will, Kate Pettigrew has made a splen-
did match.

CLINTON. *(Looks through door L., touching her
arm; she faces L.)* She might have fared worse.
Have you noticed her younger sister? 'Tis pity she's
so odd and distant.

MISS BARRYMORE. *(Catty)* The Pettigrew Cinderella?

CLINTON. *(Crosses and opens door, as they go
out R.)* Cinderella at the ball, tonight! *(Both start
to exit R.)* She's dancing with the fairy prince!
*(They go out R. as DUCHESS OF DEVONSHIRE enters
from the drawing-room, magnificently dressed, beautiful and distinguished, aged twenty-seven, followed
by LADY ANNE, who is beautifully dressed.)*

LADY ANNE. *(Agitated, following the DUCHESS)*
'Tis full twenty minutes, Duchess, since I sent my
son down to entice His Royal Highness upstairs.

DUCHESS. *(Fanning herself, walks to C.)* Compose yourself, Lady Anne, these fat German prince-
lings poison any entertainment. Be content with the
honor of his presence among your bottles. *(With a
wave of her fan, she crosses to straight-backed chair
L. and sits facing audience.)*

LADY ANNE. *(Sits after DUCHESS, in wing chair
against L. wall below doors)* His presence anywhere
is small honor beside that of the Duchess of Devonshire.

DUCHESS. *(Turns to her)* Who would not come,
my dear, to meet your dazzling Yankee? His success
tonight will be the talk of the town tomorrow.

LADY ANNE. *(Delighted)* Oh, Duchess!

DUCHESS. His manner, his voice, his wit, have

captivated the least impressionable of our sex, and
disarmed the most critical of his own. Or so I am
informed. I would appraise for myself this odd *je ne
sais quoi*——

LADY ANNE. Oh, Duchess, our cousin is *not* odd!

DUCHESS. I hear what I hear. I *also* hear that
your Kate has not danced so much as once with her
Peter. They might be already married.

LADY ANNE. *(Flustered; rises)* Indeed no,
Madam, they *dote* upon one another.

DUCHESS. *(Laughing)* Now pray remember, you
have promised me a *tete-a-tete* with your cousin.

TOM. *(Enter* TOM R., *in conversation with* LORD
STANLEY, *Under-Secretary of the Foreign Office, a
man of about fifty, who wears an order)* He drank
"vun more," and then "anuzzer" swamped him.

STANLEY. I heard the Royal snore. But let sleep-
ing princes lie, Pettigrew, and contrive for me a
word with Mr. Standish.

TOM. *(As they cross stage, front)* If the women
will let you get near him.

DUCHESS. *(Rising and coming a step to* C. *She
and* LADY ANNE *both curtsey)* Ah, Lord Stanley!
*(Taking* STANLEY'S *left arm)* Why do you never
come to my Thursdays? *(*STANLEY *and* TOM *bow.
The* DUCHESS *moves to* L .*and* STANLEY *and* DUCH-
ESS *go out* L.*)*

STANLEY. The outbreak of peace—*(With a laugh
as they both exit into ballroom Left)*—my dear
Duchess, has redoubled our labors at the Foreign
Office.

LADY ANNE. *(Following the* DUCHESS *to* L. *and
turning to* TOM *at* L.C.*)* Why have you not brought
up the Duke as I bade you?

TOM. Would you have me carry him up, ma'am?
He's snoring by the punch bowl.

LADY ANNE. Then, Thomas, someone *must* wake
him.

TOM. *(Shocked)* What, ma'am? Shake a prince of the blood by the collar?

LADY ANNE. *(Agitated, moving R. to chair between door and desk as she talks, leaving TOM L.C.)* The Duke does not so much as come up the stairs to greet his hostess. *(Moving up slightly)* 'Tis noticed how Kate dances with every Tom, Dick and Harry but not with Peter. *(Turns; comes backstage C.)* Helen will not be commonly civil to Mr. Throstle. Oh, I am distracted! *(Looks out door L.)* There's Miss Sinclair. Ask her for a dance. (THROSTLE *enters quickly from L.)*

TOM. She's an heiress; she'll not look at me. (THROSTLE *comes to* LADY ANNE, *Center; points L. and says "Ma'am!" as* TOM *goes out L.)*

LADY ANNE. Surely, sir, you would have Helen be civil to her cousin?

THROSTLE. *(Both U.C.)* Any woman here would gladly relieve her of that task. Excepting Miss Pettigrew, who seems to avoid him.

LADY ANNE. *(Disturbed; crossing to doors at L.)* Nonsense. Kate is fulfilling her social duties. *(Turns and faces him)* And if Helen is coy and shy, 'tis merely that she would tease you, dear sir. (THROSTLE *takes a step toward her, as though to say "Ma'am!")* But I will speak to her. (LADY ANNE *goes off L.* THROSTLE *watches off L. a moment, then turns up R.C.)*

*(Enter* TOM L. *MUSIC stops. Slight APPLAUSE, then VOICES heard through this scene.)*

TOM. *(Walking up to* THROSTLE, *who is up R.C.)* Did you see that, Throstle? Some insolent Scotch puppy whipped her off right in front of my very nose! But 'tis all one, for I could never bring myself to bed with that Sinclair filly, had she twice five thousand a year. *(Points off through double doors*

L.) My God, Throstle, look at him! Now the dance has stopped they all crowd around him—a levee, by God, a levee!

THROSTLE. Mr. Standish, sir, is a man of rare parts.

TOM. Too rare, by half. 'Tis no small honor for a Yankee to enter White's Club. He patronizes all the bucks, sir. Told me the best quality in England were vulgar, brutal and dirty. He turned his back on the Prince of Wales! Thank God 'twas thought an accident!

THROSTLE. *(Both are* C.*)* Why did he do so?

TOM. Because His Highness blew his nose with his fingers.

THROSTLE. Sir, the first gentleman of Europe, in his cups, is something coarse.

TOM. *(Turns; walks to desk)* So, but he's the Prince!

THROSTLE. How the man bewilders me! His strange zest for things we despise, his aversions! They are pulling down some houses built in the dark ages, on the old city wall, near Moorgate. Mr. Standish would have them preserved! I informed him these are eyesores, since the taste of our ancestors was in all respects barbarous. He was angry. He said, "How the future will curse you!" *(*TOM *yawns.)* "Whatever the taste of the future," I replied, " 'twill not be for the works of our half-savage forbears." A neat retort, I think.

TOM. We make him pay for his airs, at the gaming tables.

THROSTLE. And his ignorance of all the petty details of everyday life, and his nice disgust with so many of them!

TOM. Disgust! The young rebel! *(Turns again to* THROSTLE, *behind settee.)*

THROSTLE. We affect him as a tribe of barbarians

would affect us. Yet he's an American, a Colonial—
'tis the most absurd paradox.

Tom. The most absurd impudence. And his
damned superiority! Every morning two maids have
to carry buckets of hot water up three pairs of stairs
for Master Colonial to wash himself.

Throstle. *(Comes down a step in astonishment)*
Wash himself all over?

Tom. Every morning.

Throstle. *(Wonderingly)* Washes himself all
over, every morning!

(Kate *and* Lady Anne *enter* l. Major Clinton
*enters* r. Tom *and* Throstle *have worked up*
c. *by this time.*)

Lady Anne. Ah, Major Clinton! *(Curtsey, then
a step up as she introduces* Kate*)* Kate, this is
Peter's dear friend, Major Clinton; Mr. Throstle,
Major Clinton. (Kate *curtseys;* Clinton *bows,
holds his position.* Kate *comes to him at settee as he
exchanges bows with* Throstle.*)*

Clinton. All my congratulations, Miss Pettigrew.
You have monopolized Standish so that I have seen
nothing of him since we landed. (Kate *sits* l. *on
settee.* Clinton *sits* r. Tom *comes behind settee as
he speaks.* Lady Anne *is still behind it and to* Tom's
r. Throstle *comes down to her* l.*)*

Tom. *(To* Throstle*)* This is too good to waste
on you—they must all hear it. *(To others)* You
haven't heard this one, ma'am, nor you, Kate. Yesterday, after dinner at White's, he said he couldn't
afford to lose a hundred and twelve guineas at a sitting. He'd never lost more than fifty! Last night
three of us sat down at ecarte, and when the reckon-
ing came—zounds, it gave me a turn!

Kate. He'd lost the hundred and twelve guineas.

Tom. How did you guess? Exactly a hundred

and twelve! And he paid us off with a damned sheepish smile at me, as if to say he was sorry he'd mentioned it *before* it happened.

LADY ANNE. *(Irritated)* A truce to these childish riddles and puzzles.

CLINTON. *(To* KATE*)* You appear distressed, Miss Pettigrew. *(To others)* 'Twas but a prank; he seems to be playing some singular charade here on London.

TOM. *(Mockingly crosses to* R.*)* A woman may well mislike to live with a man who knows what she's going to do the day after tomorrow, eh, Kate? *(Exit* TOM R.*)*

LADY ANNE. *(Indignantly)* Thomas! *(Speaks in undertone with* THROSTLE *as she goes to fireplace with him)* Mr. Throstle, I must tell you—— *(Goes into whisper.)*        *(WARN Music.)*

CLINTON. *(To* KATE, *taking* TOM'S *exit for a cue to speak)* Standish has made a model of an engine that he says will drive looms by water power. He will transform England, if this be true.

*(Enter* PETER *with* LORD STANLEY L. *As* STANLEY *talks, they walk* L.C. *and stop.* KATE *and* CLINTON *listening.)*

STANLEY. *(Downstage of* PETER*)* Well, well, sir, I trust you can sympathize with the feelings of Englishmen who have been obliged to sign away a continent.

PETER. *(Both are down* C.*)* Do not grudge us our poor stretches of wilderness, my lord, you upon whose Empire the sun never sets!

STANLEY. *(Greatly impressed)* Sir, that is the most magnificent compliment ever paid to Great Britain!

PETER. It's not a bad phrase, is it? Though it might sound hackneyed if you'd heard it a hundred times before. *(Exeunt* LADY ANNE *and* THROSTLE L.)*

STANLEY. Were it not your own, sir, we should all have heard it before. After all, why did we quarrel about tea? We would have yielded the tax to end the fighting—I cannot understand why you went on with the war. *(MUSIC starts.)*

PETER. Why, my lord, to make the world safe for democracy! *(Moving over to* KATE. *Exit* STANLEY L. CLINTON *rises; steps back* R. *of settee.)* We haven't danced yet, Kate. Do you think you could bear with my clumsy steps?

CLINTON. *(Hearty, but astonished)* What, no word for me? *(*PETER *looks at him blankly.)*

KATE. Surely, Peter, you remember Major Clinton?

PETER. Oh, of course.

CLINTON. Another of his jests. My friend of twenty-seven days in the *General Wolfe* pretends he doesn't know me!

PETER. *(Hastily)* When you put off your service uniform and dress like a peacock, your own mother wouldn't know you, Clinton. You don't seem the same man ashore.

CLINTON. *(Gaping)* You took the very words out of my mouth. *You* don't seem the same man, on shore.

PETER. I've been getting my land legs. *(*PETER *steps to* KATE, *offers his arm, saying, "Kate." She rises as though to take it, then impulsively turns to* CLINTON, *saying:)*

KATE. Forgive me, Peter, I promised this dance to Major Clinton. *(*CLINTON *looks at her, astonished, then offers his arm and they go off* L. PETER, *much disturbed, standing before settee staring after them, then crosses toward window up* R. LADY ANNE *appears in doorway* L. *She steps about six feet into room and above door as she calls:)*

LADY ANNE. *(Calls)* Peter! *(The DUCHESS enters and crosses LADY ANNE, meeting PETER about* L.C. PETER *crosses to them, meeting the DUCHESS* L.C.*)* The Duchess of Devonshire, Mr. Peter Standish. *(LADY ANNE curtseys as the DUCHESS crosses her; and exits immediately. PETER bows. DUCHESS curtseys; she turns as if to go into drawing-room.)*

PETER. Ah, Duchess, I'm afraid I have already disgraced myself as a dancer. And I had three lessons! *(DUCHESS laughs; turns from door. They move across to* R. *as she says chaffingly:)*

DUCHESS. What was it you said about your American "steps"?

PETER. Oh, we have forgotten your polite measures; *our* dances are modelled on those of the— Red Indians.

DUCHESS. *(Turning at* R.C., *near settee)* If you are to take my scalp it must be by your wit, which they say is better than your dancing. I am told, sir— *(Sits settee* R.*)*—that you seem to regard this country as a museum, and ourselves as specimens in glass cases.

PETER. *(Standing to* R. *of small stool)* Oh, I cannot leave you with that absurd impression.

DUCHESS. Do your best to make another, then. *(Fusses with* R. *side of dress)* But, please, no politics; I should be no match for you there. *(To* PETER*)* You have overwhelmed Lord Stanley.

PETER. Upon one theme, in *your* company, I might do justice to what Lady Anne expects of me.

DUCHESS. Your tone of voice identifies the theme! If we are not to speak of sentiment, let me congratulate you. Miss Pettigrew will make you a devoted wife.

PETER. There is nothing in the world like the devotion of a married woman. It's a thing no married man knows anything about.

DUCHESS. What! A cynic about marriage before you have reached the altar?

PETER. What is a cynic, Duchess?

DUCHESS. *(Out front)* One who sneers at love, at romance.

PETER. Yes; one who knows the price of everything, and the value of nothing! (DUCHESS *looks at him.*) But we should face the facts. *(Sits on stool)* In love one first deceives oneself and then others— and that is what is called romance.

DUCHESS. Sir, such views of romance are commonly entertained by that most ignoble work of God, a faithless husband.

PETER. Fidelity is a strange thing! When we were young we try to be faithful, and cannot; when we are old we try to be faithless——

DUCHESS. *(Delighted)* And cannot! Oh, a delightful aphorism, sir! Your American pyrotechnics make me feel as stupid as a schoolgirl at her first ball. I can scarcely believe that I am—well, who I am——

PETER. *(Rises and with a deep bow)* Georgiana, Duchess of Devonshire!

DUCHESS. You roll it out as though you were announcing me at Court. *(MUSIC stops.)*

PETER. *(With real but wholly impersonal enthusiasm)* All the charm of the period seems to center in that name!

DUCHESS. Flatterer! Admit that in America you had never heard of me!

PETER. What barbarian has not heard of the Fifth Duchess? *(Sits again on stool)* Your name in English social history is the finest flower of the age of elegance. We know your face from—— *(Anxiously)* Gainsborough *has* painted you, hasn't he? *(She nods)* All the legend and beauty of the age cling about you. All one's dreams of the time have you for their central figure—your receptions, those dinners at Devonshire House—as powerful in politics as irresistible in love. What can the eighteenth century offer that—*(Breaks off, alarmed, continues self-consciously)*—that can compare with——

DUCHESS. *(Coldly)* You speak of me so strangely. *(With a little nervous laugh)* I find your overwhelming compliments—a little disturbing. You're talking about me as we two might talk about Madame de Maintenon. In the past tense!

PETER. Oh, no, Duchess, I never once used the past tense! *(He rises.)*

DUCHESS. You have been *thinking* of me in the past tense. *(She rises. Front)* Now I know what it is! *(Turns slowly to face him)* You've been talking about me—as though—— *(She steps back)* —as though I were already dead!

PETER. *(Discouraged)* And I tried so hard to make an impression.

DUCHESS. *(Controlling herself and smiling)* Sir, *you* have made an—indescribable impression. *(The DUCHESS curtseys, turns, exits R., as THROSTLE enters L. and crosses to PETER. MUSIC starts.)*

THROSTLE. *(C.)* Sir, my compliments upon your success tonight.

PETER. *(L.C., looking off R.)* My success with the Duchess has been devastating. *(Sits on settee)* Is Major Clinton in there?

THROSTLE. *(Takes step back, looking L.)* He's dancing again with Miss Pettigrew.

PETER. Oh, damn the meddler! I wish they'd order him abroad again.

THROSTLE. *(L.C.)* Sir, you appear distressed. Ah, believe me, I've known Miss Pettigrew these five years; 'tis but a mood.

PETER. Your assurance is most comforting.

THROSTLE. And I entirely understand about Miss Helen.

PETER. What do you mean?

"Berkeley Square"

Act III, See Page 98

THROSTLE. *(Pleasantly)* Merely that I take no exception to your marked attentions to the lady to whom I offer the devotion of a lifetime.

PETER. *(Angry)* Come, Throstle, you're not fifty. I advise you not to offer any young girl the devotion of a lifetime until you're over seventy.

THROSTLE. *(Paling)* Your self-assurance, sir, is magnificent. Are you so confident that Miss Pettigrew is not almost of a mind to break with you?

PETER. *(Laughing, with a touch of nervous hysteria)* Kate, break with me! *(Rises, standing before settee)* Listen, Throstle! We're going to get married and have three children—one of them dies of smallpox at the age of seven and is buried in St. Mark's Churchyard! That's absurd, isn't it? But you believe it, don't you?

THROSTLE. *(Keeps composure with difficulty)* Since you can read Miss Pettigrew's future, perhaps you'll inform me as to Miss Helen's?

PETER. *(Staggered)* Helen's future. No, I don't know that! *(Turning up by L., moves around settee almost to desk, then turns and comes to back of settee. With forced jocularity)* Look here, Throstle, can't you take a joke? I don't know any more about the future than you do.

THROSTLE. *(Takes snuff; turns away)* My reason, sir, tells me as much.

TOM. *(Enters R. At door)* Gad's life, Throstle, he's still asleep! *(MUSIC stops.)*

PETER. Who's asleep?

TOM. His Royal Highness!

PETER. Why not let him sleep?

THROSTLE. Ah, you wouldn't know, sir; etiquette permits no guest to leave any assembly before Royalty.

PETER. *(Laughs; turns upstage)* Then this ball will have to go on all night?

TOM. 'Tis no laughing matter, sir. (PETER *walks*

*back to portrait up stage R.; looks at it; looks out
of R. window.* CLINTON *enters L., talking to* STAN-
LEY. *They stop about L.C.* STANLEY *above* CLIN-
TON.)

CLINTON. Gad, sir, as I tried to force myself
through the press, I saw a fellow running away with
a piece of charred bone.

THROSTLE. *(Walks up to them)* Charred bone?

CLINTON. *(Taking* TOM *and* PETER *into scene)*
Did any of you see that woman burned before New-
gate this morning?

PETER. *(Startled. Comes diagonally down to R.C.)*
What woman burned?

CLINTON. *(Standing L., below and L. of* LORD
STANLEY) One Phoebe Harris, for coining. There's
not been such a crush for years—I paid three guineas
for a seat in a window.

THROSTLE. *(With a faint sneer)* Those who
fancy the odor of burning flesh may observe the
roasting of an ox in the Smithfields Market any
morning, gratis.

PETER. *(Walks to stool beside settee. Exploding)*
You paid three guineas for a seat in a window to
see a woman burned alive? And that can happen
in London?

TOM. *(Who has been sitting L. arm of settee, rises
and takes a step down R.)* They strangle 'em before
they put the fire to the wood.

PETER. *(To* CLINTON. *Sits settee)* I hope you
enjoyed the spectacle! Did you take your mother
and sisters?

TOM. *(Shocked)* Sir, women of quality do not
attend executions.

CLINTON. *(With faint sneer)* Americans appear
squeamish people—when they're not at home——
(LORD STANLEY *pats* CLINTON *on shoulder.*)

THROSTLE. *(C., interrupting tactfully, to* PETER)
I trust, sir, our great lexicographer did not disap-

point you when you called upon him this afternoon?

CLINTON. *(To* PETER*)* I saw Doctor Johnson this morning, at the spectacle which so offends you.

PETER. So he was there too, was he? God!

TOM. What did the old bear say to you?

*(WARN Music.)*

PETER. Oh, he thundered out a few platitudes. Really, his friends ought to stop him from dribbling food and snuff all over his waistcoat. And he'd be none the worse for a bath.

TOM. *(Crosses* PETER *to* CLINTON *and* STANLEY *at fireplace)* Bath! You and your everlasting baths!

PETER. Bathing hasn't always been an eccentricity —you admire the Romans; the Romans bathed.

THROSTLE. *(L.C.)* Only excessively, sir, when they became degenerate. The virile fathers of the Republic——

PETER. *(Interrupting impatiently. Rising)* Were as dirty as you are? I suppose you're right.

TOM. 'Struth, sir, you speak of the best of us here as no better than a litter of lousy Irishmen.

CLINTON. *(Comes* C.*)* What in the devil's name is all this about baths? You took but one bath in the *General Wolfe,* and you talked about that for a week beforehand.

PETER. *(At fault for a moment)* I can't stand salt water. *(Walks toward window* R.*, looks at portrait, turns and comes* R. *front, meeting* HELEN *as she enters* R. *MUSIC starts.)*

CLINTON. *(As they move to door* L.*,* THROSTLE *behind* TOM *and* CLINTON*)* What *have* you done to him here?

TOM. There's no fine lady so finicky as this Colonial. You didn't tell me he was like this, Clinton! *(Starts to exit into ballroom* L.*)*

CLINTON. *(Explosively—follows* TOM *off* L. *as he speaks)* Gad, sir, he wasn't. London has made another man of him. It is altogether incredible!

(THROSTLE *turns at the door and watches* PETER *and* HELEN. LORD STANLEY *is standing above* THROSTLE *at door* L. *and talks to* THROSTLE.)

PETER. *(Standing with* HELEN *before settee)* He's been annoying you again. If only I could *do* something about it.

HELEN. But you do *do* something, just by feeling as you *do.* Are we going to dance again? (DUCHESS *enters* R., *crossing to* STANLEY, *up* L.C. *Almost lose this speech)* All the other women will be so jealous!

PETER. *(Almost lose this speech)* The Duchess tells me I dance so badly.

DUCHESS. *(Speaks as she enters)* I'm bored beyond all endurance, Stanley, and I've sent for my carriage.

STANLEY. But His Highness!

DUCHESS. Oh, I've no desire to make scandal by leaving before Royalty, so there's naught for it but to wake up the drunken old pig and get him out of the house. *(Sees* PETER *as she is crossing down* R.; *hesitates for just a moment, then sweeps from room)* Come, lend me your countenance! *(The* DUCHESS *exits* R., *followed by* LORD STANLEY.)

HELEN. What *have* you been saying to the Duchess, Peter? She's been repeating such wicked, hard, cruel things downstairs——

PETER. Come and talk to me. (HELEN *sits on settee.* THROSTLE *exit* L.) Your mother begged me to impress the Duchess—*(Sitting on stool)*—so I dazzled her with some cheap epigrams made up by a fellow named Oscar Wilde.

HELEN. A friend of yours in New York?

PETER. Oh, no. He's dead. At least he's not been—— Well, never mind. It's rather complicated.

HELEN. You did indeed dazzle the Duchess, Peter. But somehow you seem to have made her almost afraid of you, too!

PETER. I know. They all like me at first. But

then I say something—wrong. I see it in their eyes. *(Intensely; leaning toward her)* Are you afraid of me?

HELEN. I couldn't be afraid of somebody I'm sorry for.

PETER. *(Suspicious)* Why are you sorry for me?

HELEN. Oh, because I think you're unhappy with us, though you're so brave, and you try to hide it. You feel so strange here——

PETER. Yes, I do.

HELEN. I can't imagine what America's like. It's so far away. But I suppose everything's so different. And the people, too.

PETER. Yes, that's it. Everything's different. Oh, you are so kind!

HELEN. And as for what worries you so, people being afraid of you, I mean—that's only—only——

PETER. Only what?

HELEN. You know, Peter. It's because you look through us, you seem to know what we think, even what we're going to do next. *(Slowly)* I don't understand you. And I wish I could help you.

PETER. Oh, but you do! Just by your sympathy, even though you can't know how much I need it. The days are all right. I go about your old London —that's the most wonderful experience that ever came to a living man! But when I lie in bed and think! It all seems nightmare, until I remember you. You're not like the others. You're—real—— *(Seizes her hand.)*

HELEN. *(Withdrawing hand and turning, slightly, from him)* I am Kate's sister! *(MUSIC stops.)*

DUKE. *(Off stage R.)* Dot vos witty, Duchess— yes? *(DUKE laughs heartily.)*

PETER. *(Humbly)* Forgive me.

*(LORD STANLEY enters R. and crosses the stage hurriedly, with the air of a man with a mission. He*

*ignores* PETER *and* HELEN. *As he crosses he beckons to* LADY ANNE, *who enters from* L., *followed by* THROSTLE, *who stops down* L.; *then* MISS BARRYMORE *and* CLINTON, *who stand above* L. *door, before* STANLEY *has fully crossed stage. The voices of the* DUKE *and* DUCHESS *are heard.* PETER *and* HELEN *rise as they enter* R. *The* DUKE *is elderly, many-chinned, amiable. He wears the Garter with ribbon and star.)*

DUKE. *(Laughing)* The Duke of Cumberland must not be known as the Duke of Slumberland. *(As the* DUKE *passes the settee the* DUCHESS *crosses rear of it to up* L.C., *where she joins* LORD STANLEY.) Zo, goot efening, Laty Anne.

LADY ANNE. *(C.—curtseys)* Your Royal Highness confers a great honor upon us. *(Enter* L. KATE *and* TOM. ALL *gradually spreading out in a semicircle,* TOM *and* KATE L., *downstage.)*

DUKE. Your bunch iss fery goot. I haf stayed too long, pelow. I asg your pardon. *(LADY ANNE curtseys again and says "Your Royal Highness!" Looking over company)* I had hert mine ald vrent Sir Choshwa Reynolds vas here.

LADY ANNE. *(Embarrassed)* He was suddenly taken ill, Your Highness.

DUKE. Zo? I am sorry. And vere iss diss Amerigan gousin off whom I haf hert? *(LADY ANNE gestures to* PETER, *who advances and bows.)*

*(WARN Curtain.)*

LADY ANNE. Your Royal Highness, Mr. Peter Standish.

DUKE. You marry Miss Bettigrew, Mr. Standish?

PETER. Yes, Your Highness.

DUKE. Vere iss she? *(LADY ANNE moves* L. KATE *advances* LC., *front of chair down* L.C.)*

LADY ANNE. My daughter, Your Royal Highness. (KATE *curtseys.*)

DUKE. Zo! A fine bair of lofers. All my gongratulations. (PETER *bows.* KATE *curtseys again. To* PETER) You haf gum a long joorney—Amerigans are great dravellers. You haf drabbled mooch, Mr. Standish?

PETER. *(Casually)* Oh, from time to time. (DUCHESS, *who has been standing to* R., *rear of* DUKE L., *moves toward him and signals him a reminder with her fan.*)

DUKE. *(Taking the hint, with a laugh)* Zo! Laty Anne, the Tuchess has tolt me it is fery late. I must dake my leaf. (LADY ANNE *curtseys; the* DUKE *bows to her and to the others; turns; takes* PETER'S *arm*) You trink mooch in Ameriga—an Indian trink, I haf hert. *(As the* DUKE *walks* PETER *out* L. *everyone curtseys.*)

PETER. Oh, you mean corn whisky, Your Highness. I found a bottle in my boxes, if you care to try it.

DUKE. And how did you get it t'rough the gustoms?

*(Exeunt* DUKE *and* PETER L., LADY ANNE *immediately following, with all the others excepting* HELEN *and* KATE. *As they all start the LIGHTS dim rapidly and the curtain falls rapidly. It is down only about ten seconds.)*

## QUICK CURTAIN

## ACT TWO

Scene II. At Rise: Helen *is up* l., *looking out windows.* Kate *is in chair down* l.c.

Helen. The last carriage is gone. (Kate *buries her head on her arm, sitting on chair* l.c.) What is it, Kate? We always tell one another everything.

Kate. Helen dear, I don't know myself. I *meant* to dance with him—I was rude, ill-bred, anything you like—but I *couldn't*.

Helen. He cannot understand why you slight him. (*They walk to settee.*)

Kate. Then you were talking of me as you danced. (*Ironically*) I suppose he complained of my cruelty. (Helen *sits on settee;* Kate *on stool.*)

Helen. He doesn't seem to take your behavior—so seriously as I do.

Kate. Oh, so he doesn't take me seriously?

Helen. He says there can't be any *real* disagreement. It isn't possible, because of course you *will* marry.

Kate. So; he thinks I *must* marry him, because we must have the money!

Helen. (*Impulsively*) Oh, Kate, you *know* such a thought could never cross his mind!

Kate. How do you know what thoughts cross his mind? About you, for instance? You're too good, Helen, to suspect anybody.

Helen. (*Indignant*) Suspect Peter? Of what?

Kate. Oh, it doesn't matter.

72

HELEN. *(Earnestly)* I want to compose this—estrangement. I shall be miserable until everything is settled—and over.

KATE. You think I'm being very unfair. But there's such a thing as instinct, Helen.

HELEN. Oh, Kate, just because he sees and knows things, strangely——

KATE. *(Interrupts)* I can't help it, Helen. When I'm with him he makes me afraid. *(Rises)* And when you're with him—I'm afraid for you!

LADY ANNE. *(Enters L., followed by* THROSTLE. KATE *walks above settee to up* R.C. LADY ANNE *walks* R.; *sits on settee by* HELEN*)* The dear, dear Duchess! Had she not awakened him, he might have slept on for hours, everyone cooped up here, and our ball the laughing-stock of London!

THROSTLE. *(Up stage* L.C.; *with bow to* KATE, *who is up* R.C.*)* Miss Pettigrew, your lover has the town at his feet.

LADY ANNE. Oh, dear, kind sir, your partiality—

THROSTLE. Has not obscured my judgment. *(With veiled irony)* None of your guests could credit our late Colonies with such a product.

TOM. *(Enters* L., *yawning; sits chair down* L.*)* Look ye, Throstle, 'twas you took my cousin to Sir Joshua.

THROSTLE. I did, sir.

TOM. Sir Joshua sends Mr. Standish his compliments by me, and would have Mr. Standish destroy the portrait; he'll paint him no more!

LADY ANNE. *(Astonished)* What can Sir Joshua mean? Our cousin was to sit for him here tomorrow.

TOM. Then he may sit and admire himself, for there will be no painter.

KATE. *(Crosses down a step)* I wonder why!

TOM. *(Sits in chair beside her)* A hundred guineas they compounded for, and now the man throws picture and money too into Standish's face!

THROSTLE. *(As he crosses to easel)* Some fault in the portrait has displeased the artist.

TOM. *(Insinuating)* Fault in the portrait, eh? *(All look at* TOM *except* THROSTLE. THROSTLE *drags out easel from behind writing-desk, turns it around. It is about half finished.* KATE *up stage* C. THROSTLE *turns and comes down* L.C.; *looks at picture.)*

THROSTLE. The work is in the artist's best manner.

KATE. *(Walks up to and gazes intently at picture)* I wonder why!

THROSTLE. *(Taking snuff)* This is not like Sir Joshua.

KATE. *(Turning to* TOM) What exactly *did* Sir Joshua say?

TOM. *(Mimicing Reynolds)* "There is a quality in his every look, when I take up my brushes and fasten my eyes on his face, beyond all *my* experience of human nature."

KATE. *(Slowly)* Painters have good eyes.

TOM. He had no mind to set his on Peter again.

KATE. *(As to herself)* What did he see? *(Walks* R. *front; sits on stool.)*

HELEN. *(Rising and taking her arm)* Sister, what is it?

LADY ANNE. Kate, Kate, what is amiss with you?

TOM. Vapours, vapours.

THROSTLE. *(Who has remained standing* L.C. *Disturbed)* None of us understand him.

HELEN. *(With spirit)* I understand him—he's strange here. He feels just the same way, about us, that some of us do about him.

TOM. *(Bored, puts feet upon other chair)* Why shouldn't he understand us? We are but ordinary people of quality.

KATE. God knows what he is.

LADY ANNE. *(Angrily)* Shame, shame, to speak so of your lover!

TOM. 'Tis no matter; perhaps Yankees get like that.

HELEN. Oh, Tom!

KATE. *(Outburst)* While you can pigeon him at White's you'll choke it down. But what of me?

LADY ANNE. *(Rising)* Kate! This is disgraceful!

KATE. So his bank account be sound, naught else matters to anyone—but me.

HELEN. *(Distressed)* Kate, Kate, don't you see that he's unhappy, too?

LADY ANNE. *(Interrupts, to KATE)* I forbid you to discuss your lover so.

MAID. *(Appears in door L. with candle-snuffer)* The musicians, my lady.

LADY ANNE. *(Sweeping L., crossing in front of THROSTLE)* Tom, this is your mischief, with your tales to fright scullery maids! *(LADY ANNE walks out with MAID L., giving directions.)*

KATE. How did he first get into this house?

TOM. I'll engage his legs carried him.

KATE. He walked in here. No one saw him below. You remember the rain. His boots were dry.

HELEN. *(Standing before settee, trying to reassure her)* Kate, dear, what *do* you mean?

KATE. I don't know what I mean. I think I'm going out of my senses.

HELEN. There's no reason to be afraid of him.

KATE. *(Front)* There's no reason to be afraid of a graveyard at midnight.

THROSTLE. *(Moving to TOM, agitated)* And we're living in the eighteenth century! *(Comes down, showing he wishes to sit in chair by TOM. TOM removes feet from it. THROSTLE dusts chair with handkerchief before sitting, then takes snuff)* The age of reason, the age of Voltaire!

HELEN. What if he does see things—ahead of other people?

KATE. *(More intensely)* How did he get into this house?

HELEN. Oh, that again!

KATE. *(To everyone)* Nobody answers me.

HELEN. Kate, dearest, you *shall* be happy. Ask him about whatever troubles you!

KATE. I loved him, when he kissed me that first day. And now I'd rather die than ask him—anything!

PETER. *(Enters R.; stops at door; looks at easel.* THROSTLE *rises)* Hello, what's the picture doing out here?

TOM. Sir Joshua would have you destroy his portrait.

THROSTLE. Sir, I propose to wait upon Sir Joshua tomorrow.

PETER. *(Without surprise)* Pray do not disturb yourself.

HELEN. *(Smile)* You do not seem affronted, cousin.

PETER. He's entitled to paint whom he chooses.

KATE. *(With an effort)* You expected this?

PETER. Now that it's happened, I'm not surprised.

HELEN. 'Tis most uncivil of him, cousin. *(Enter* LADY ANNE L.)

PETER. *(Vaguely, as though to himself; slowly, as he walks to easel, looks at portrait)* The picture shall not be destroyed, and Sir Joshua will complete it.

TOM. *(Languidly, rising)* Demnation, sir, men have sent their seconds for less than this! *(*PETER *comes behind settee.* LADY ANNE, *who has been standing* L.C., *comes* C. TOM *is down* L.)*

LADY ANNE. What! Still harping on that portrait! An old man's vagary, dear cousin; he'll no doubt send you his apologies; but, if not, Mr. Gains-

borough will do you a better likeness. *(Goes to door*
R.*)* Thomas, put the ugly thing back where it came
from.

TOM. *(As he goes to easel)* Gad's life! All these
frenzies about a lump of paint! (TOM *lugs easel
back and stows it behind writing-bureau.)*

LADY ANNE. Cousin, I've had no time for a mor-
sel of supper, nor, I am sure, have you. Come below. 'Tis late. Come, Mr. Throstle. Come down
with Helen. *(Exits R. TOM exits after LADY ANNE.)*

(THROSTLE *walks to settee;* HELEN *rises, takes his
arm; they go out the door R. PETER, above settee, watches HELEN exit. KATE sees PETER
watching HELEN and rises and crosses to door
R.C.; closes it, leaning against it, looking at
PETER intently.)*

PETER. *(Crosses down R.C.)* Kate, what's the matter? You've been avoiding me all the evening.

KATE. You have not been avoiding my sister.

PETER. That fellow Clinton's been upsetting you,
hasn't he? I know what he told you.

KATE. *(Begins to drive a bit)* Of course you
know what he told me.

PETER. You see, Kate——

KATE. *(Interrupting)* You know what he told
me. You know what I am thinking now. You know
what is going to happen next.

PETER. *(Steps nearer to her, then looks away)*
This is just a mood, Kate; it will pass. (KATE *shud-
ders; moves back.)* There's nothing to be afraid of.
                                                    *(WARN Wind.)*

KATE. *I thought I loved you.*

PETER. *(Definitively)* You mustn't talk like that.
We're going to be married!

KATE. *(Takes a step away from door)* So, I am

to marry you, when I am put to it to force myself to
remain alone with you!

PETER. Oh, this is that cursed picture—— *(Looks
toward easel.)*

KATE. Sir Joshua saw it! *(Moves toward door* R.)

PETER. (KATE *comes to his vision again. He is
down* C.) Go to bed, Kate; you'll be yourself again
in the morning.

KATE. *(Turns at door)* In the morning I shall
post to Budleigh. I cannot stay in this house with
you. *(Tries to slip bracelet from wrist.)*

PETER. *(Coming around settee to front and* L. *of
it)* Kate, you mustn't break our engagement. *(Con-
fidently)* You *can't* do that! You didn't do that!
*(WIND heard outside.)*

KATE. *(Her self-control breaking down)* Oh, I
*can't* do that. How smugly you say it! So you think
there are no limits to what a wizard can do with a
woman? The women all press after you, don't they?
But no woman wishes to dance with you twice—
excepting Helen! I was never so afraid of anything
in my life as I am of you—*(Laughs wildly)*—and
you think you can make me marry you when I fear
you as I fear the devil! *(Throws bracelet on floor.)*

PETER. This can't be!

KATE. I leave London in the morning, and I'll not
return while you are in this house. *(Backs a step)*
I hope I may never set eyes on you again. In God's
name, go back to—to America, if that's where you
come from!

PETER. But things *can't* happen that *didn't* happen.

KATE. *(Front)* You speak words without sense.
Only God and the devil know what they mean.
*(Starts for door* R.)

PETER. Oh, Kate, be reasonable. (KATE *turns on
him.)* Please. I only mean it's all arranged. *I've
come over to marry you*—we are going to be mar-

ried, and live in this house. That happens! *(Pleadingly)* You must feel that just as I do, don't you? It's *true!* (KATE *turns to go.* PETER *takes a step toward her—hysterically)* No, Kate, don't go! *(She turns to him)* We'll be happy together, and this marriage *has* to be. It *is! (Points to bracelet) This, this* is impossible! You *can't* do that! *(Turning away a pace to* L.) It *didn't happen* that way!

KATE. *(Facing him as she stands down* R.) I've only this to say to you: I shall not return from Budleigh while *you* are in this house! *(Turns and starts to open door* R. *WIND stops dead.)*

PETER. *(Sudden realization)* Wait! While I am in this house! *(Speaks directly to her. She stops and faces him)* Kate, that will be all right. You and—I—will be happy together. *(She has hand on door)* Kate! You won't go to Budleigh tomorrow, for when you meet me in the morning I shall be— different. I won't seem the same man. I may feel differently about Helen and Throstle. Promise me now that you'll stand by Helen against them all, even against—me. Help her, Kate! She'll be alone, and she'll need your help——

KATE. She will indeed need help if *you* take such an interest in her! *(Exits* R., *closing door.)*

(PETER *walks to door after her as she shuts it. He turns, looks at the bracelet, walking in a straight line to* C.; *turns, looks at portrait, walks up to it, then sits in chair before window* L., *half collapsing.* MAID *enters* L., *turns and snuffs candles 1 and 2. As she turns to snuff candles 3 and 4 on other side of door,* PETER *rises, takes step toward fire and looks at her. She hesitates, as though afraid, but he turns, looks up at tapestry panel as he passes it, goes to window* R., *and, with one knee on window-seat, looks out.* MAID *snuffs candles 3 and 4, crosses before fire, snuffs*

*candles 5 and 6, comes down to before console
table on way to snuff other candles, but* PETER
*rises, turns from window, looks through her.
She is afraid of him, and she turns and goes out
L., carrying snuffer, looking back at him over
her shoulder from door. As* MAID *goes out door.
WIND starts. Count of eight. THUNDER
starts softly as* PETER *gets near door. Both
NOISES increase, reach their height and stop
dead as* HELEN *opens the door* R. PETER *walks
c., turns, looks at easel again, his back to audience; walks to tapestry, then turns and walks,
slowly and stiffly as though dazed, toward door
R. When he is about six feet from the door it
opens suddenly and* HELEN *enters, flurried, as
though she had been running. He halts. She
closes door and stands with her back to it.)*

HELEN.  Peter!

PETER.  *(At length, in dazed voice)*  You know?

HELEN.  We all know.  *(He turns; walks* L.C.*)*
Kate's not herself tonight.  You mustn't think hardly
of her, cousin.

PETER.  *(Turns, standing* L.C.*)*  Oh, it isn't Kate's
fault.

HELEN.  That's generous of you, Peter.  I want
you to tell me what all this mystery means, so that
I can go to Kate——

PETER.  *(Crosses to* L. *of her)*  No, I can't; you'd
be afraid of me, too.

HELEN.  *(With quiet dignity and force)*  That's
not true!

PETER.  *(Sits on stool.* HELEN *is just* R. *of it)*
Oh, if I could only believe that!

HELEN.  *(Gently pressing)*  How can you speak
of things that haven't happened yet, as though they
had happened?  How can you know things you
couldn't know?  First, about my shawl.  And since,

so many things? (HELEN *sits on settee.*) Tell me!
*(Pause.)*

PETER. The border-line between what's just happened, and what's just going to is—shadowy, for me.
Things of tomorrow often seem as real as things of
yesterday. And so, in fact, they are.

HELEN. Then it's true! You do see ahead!

PETER. You believe, when it's incredible, against
nature?

HELEN. Can you see ahead just a day or two, or
months and years?

PETER. Many months, and many years. *(Looking
up at her.)*

HELEN. I love life so! I want to see ahead, because I love it so.

PETER. So you're in love with the future, as I was
in love with the—— *(He breaks off)* It's better
just to dream about what's ahead—to dream *your*
dreams—than really to know.

HELEN. But, Peter, I want to make Kate understand about these powers of yours; I want to make
her see how proud and happy she should be, instead
of afraid.

PETER. *(Looking away)* She'd only be still more
afraid. It wouldn't be any use. *(Turns to her)* But
I could tell you about things that are going to happen, just for yourself, if you really want so much
to know.

HELEN. *(Eagerly)* Oh, yes, Peter, please! Things
you've seen!

PETER. Things I've seen. Where shall I begin?
Helen, you see the candle there? Well, long after
us, this room—*(With a wave of his hand toward
window)*—Berkley Square, all London outside, will
be lit by one movement of a man's hand.

HELEN. By magic? But—what will it be like,
Peter?

PETER. *(Helplessly)* I can't tell you; you wouldn't

understand; there aren't any words that could make
you understand.

HELEN. *(She is leaning forward eagerly; their
eyes meet and she continues to look at him fixedly)*
No words. There aren't any words because these
things come to your mind in visions, Peter, and I
think I could see them, too—through your eyes. Will
you let me try?

PETER. But that isn't possible.

HELEN. Let me look! *(Gazes intently into his
eyes.)*

PETER. Helen! Your eyes burn mine!

HELEN. *(In low voice)* 'Tis this room. It blazes
with your magic lights, Peter! There's your portrait, on the wall, finished! You said it would be.

PETER. The veil is thin, for you!

HELEN. A man and a girl. They are dressed—so
queerly. The man turns to her; he kisses her. I can't
see his face, but he's like you, Peter.

PETER. *(Wrenches his head away)* No, no!

HELEN. Yes, show me, I *will* see!

PETER. Not that, the wonders of the future—ah,
*now* look! *(Turns head back to her.)*

HELEN. *(Looking in his eyes again)* Sunshine,
white clouds, three great birds, bigger than a hundred eagles——

PETER. Machines, with men in them.

HELEN. And below them, water! The ocean!
That great floating mountain there! A ship? No
sails! No masts! And beyond—a great cluster of
towers. They climb into the clouds. Oh, Peter, is it
heaven?

PETER. Only a city across the sea.

HELEN. A fairy dream city. It fades. *(PETER
turns his head away. HELEN looks out front)* Is the
future all poetry, beauty? They fly like birds, crush
the ocean, their houses pierce the sky. They'll con-
quer evil. They'll be angels, not men.

PETER. *(Murmurs ironically)* "Angels, not men."
(PETER *turns his head as* HELEN *again peers into
his eyes.)* No—*(Shaking his head sadly)*—you'd see
other pictures now, things that you mustn't see.

HELEN. *(Grasps his shoulders)* I will see!

PETER. *(Moans, but turns his head to her)* You
cannot bear it!

HELEN. Monsters—no, men, in masks over their
heads—a yellow mist around them—they fall, they
twist in the mud——

PETER. *(With great effort)* If you *must* see, let
it be by night!

HELEN. Lights, dancing, flashing, everywhere!
But this is most beautiful of all.

PETER. The fireworks of hell.

HELEN. Oh! A great flame opens like a flower.

PETER. A dump of shells that blew a score of men
to pieces.

HELEN. *(Unheeding)* Curving streams of fire—

PETER. Pumped out of hoses to shrivel men up
like insects!

HELEN. *(Shrinks back; covers face with hands)*
Oh!

PETER. *(Leaping up and back behind stool)* We
should have stopped with your fairy city.

HELEN. Devils, demons, not men! *(She rises;
turns from him* R. *front)* 'Tis not true! God would
never have put us here to suffer, for a race of fiends
like that to come after us. *(Buries her face in her
hands.)*

PETER. *(Comes to her and tenderly embraces her;
they are* R. *of settee)* Helen, dear Helen, what were
we doing?

HELEN. *(She removes her hands from her eyes,
turning to* PETER*)* The mystery, behind your eyes!

PETER. You saw the future there. *(Pause.)*

HELEN. But there was something else, more wonderful than that! *(They disengage; he turns away,*

*crossing to* L.C. *She half turns away, then turns to him again.*) And now I will go to Kate and tell her that I have shared your vision, and why it is that people are afraid——

PETER. No, you mustn't tell her. She won't be afraid tomorrow. Nobody will be afraid any more. I'll be different then.

HELEN. (*Walks toward door* R.—*then turns*) But I don't understand why I mustn't talk to Kate——

PETER. You think she threw me over tonight just because she was afraid of me? It's more hopeless than that, Helen. She's found out that I don't love her.

HELEN. (*After pause*) But you want to marry her.

PETER. Don't let's talk about that. I had to go on with it, that was all.

HELEN. Then you don't love Kate any more than she loves you now, and it isn't about Kate you're unhappy, but because you feel lost here, and strange, and because people are afraid of you——

PETER. Yes, and as everything has closed in around me, your sympathy has kept me from going mad.

HELEN. You make me very happy.

PETER. You know how I feel. You must know. But try to believe, even though you can never understand why, that the beauty that is with us and about us now, though it's more lovely than all the real things that ever were, *isn't* real, Helen. It's only a mirage. It's like a vision of heaven. It couldn't exist in this world at all, or in any real world. It's—it's unnatural!

HELEN. (*Walks up to him*) Unnatural!

PETER. Yes, and impossible, *not real,* Helen. You must forget it all and forget me, for your own dear sake. (*He turns away a pace up stage to stool.*)

HELEN. You know I can't do that, Peter.

PETER. *(Sits on stool, facing to* L. *in agony and remorse)* Oh, what have I done?

HELEN. *(Bewildered, standing in front of him)* Peter, you know the future! Tell me ours!

PETER. Our future! *(Looks up at her, startled)* No, I don't know that. Oh, Helen, try to understand. I come to you from—somewhere else. Another world. *(Looking away.)*

HELEN. I know. It's all so different, here. *(LIGHTS begin to dim.)*

PETER. But I'm not—*(Rises and steps back)*—one of you!

HELEN. I've always felt that, Peter. *(Her hands go out to him)* Peter, it's something you've done that's like a wild beast in your mind. *(A thought strikes her)* Peter! What price have you paid for the splendor about you? *(Crosses to him. Makes to embrace him, but hesitates)* You've not sold your soul to——

PETER. No, my soul's not damned, not what you mean by damned. *(Embraces her)* I love you. Oh, God, help us both! I love you!

HELEN. *(Quietly and proudly)* I loved you before I ever saw you, in my first dream of you, coming with a candle, from somewhere far away, to meet me.

PETER. Oh, but, Helen, I'm not playing my part now. *(Breaks from her; moves* L. *in front of* HELEN*)* I'm myself, you see. I'm *myself,* and I'm muddling everything up! This isn't possible, this isn't my world—or yours. It isn't my life—or yours! *(Backs away from her, up* L.C., *until he is in MOONLIGHT cast through* R. *window.)*

HELEN. Then take me away with you, Peter.

PETER. I can't! I can't!

HELEN. *(With a cry. Runs to him; clings to him)* Then don't leave me!

PETER. I won't! *(Looks wildly behind him to*

*where the picture hangs in the modern scene—then kisses her)* When I kissed Kate, that was *his* kiss, to his betrothed! *(Straining her to him)* But there's never been a kiss like *that* since the world began!

## SLOW CURTAIN

# ACT THREE

Scene I: *The room in 1784. Late afternoon—a week later. The scene is set as in Act I, Scenes I and III. Both curtains are open—both windows are shut.*

*MAID shows in* THROSTLE R., *curtseys, closes door and crosses to* L. *and exits* L. THROSTLE *walks* R.C., *then back to window* R. *Enter* LADY ANNE L. THROSTLE *turns, bows to* LADY ANNE, *who moves up stage behind settee.*

THROSTLE. Your faithful servant, madam.

LADY ANNE. *(Embarrassed, curtseys up* L.C.*)* A pleasure, indeed a pleasure, dear Mr. Throstle! *(During this* TOM *has entered* L. *He and* THROSTLE *bow.* TOM *strolls to fireplace; leans on elbow against it.)*

TOM. *(Nonchalantly)* 'Pon my oath, Throstle, you haven't been near us in a week.

THROSTLE. *(Standing on* R., *halfway down stage)* I have been with you in thought.

LADY ANNE. We had hoped, sir, that your visits, so welcome always, were not now to be discontinued.

THROSTLE. In the altered circumstances, you would say, Lady Anne?

TOM. Things do turn out in devilish queer fashions.

LADY ANNE. *(Sharply)* I know of nothing, Thomas, that has turned out queerly in this house.

TOM. *(Smiling)* Mr. Throstle would scarcely agree with you there, ma'am.

LADY ANNE. *(Reprovingly)* Thomas!

THROSTLE. Nevertheless, there can be no choice between my fifteen hundred and your cousin's ten thousand a year.

TOM. *(Approvingly)* You know the world, sir!

THROSTLE. *(Walks R. front)* One corner of it, fairly well.

LADY ANNE. Dear, dear friend, such tact, such breeding—had it been anyone else—— *(Comes down to right-hand side of small table, not looking at him. Crosses to below table)* But indeed 'twas evident from the first that Helen and Mr. Standish were made for each other.

THROSTLE. *(Standing R.C.)* I have come to lay at Miss Helen's feet the felicitations of a rejected suitor.

LADY ANNE. *(Hurriedly. Turns to him)* Pray, do not do that, sir!

THROSTLE. But, ma'am, I have ears, I have eyes, and so indeed have others. *(Walks up near her, C.)* What motive can there be for reticence?

TOM. What indeed! Every tongue in London must be wagging, ma'am. Does he not avoid everyone since the ball? Are they not seen together every day? *(LADY ANNE, facing front, shows her displeasure at what TOM says.)*

LADY ANNE. *(Constrained again. Not quite looking at him)* When we have news, Mr. Throstle, you shall be the first to hear.

THROSTLE. Am I then to understand that Mr. Standish has made as yet no formal application—— *(THROSTLE is standing R.C. down stage. LADY ANNE C., below L.C. table front. HELEN enters R., followed by PETER. TOM L. back. PETER is in riding costume and carries a formidable riding-crop in left hand. PETER's face is paler and more drawn than in Act Two; he seems to have aged; he is much more nervous. As LADY ANNE goes back to TOM)* Miss

Helen, it has been a week since I have been able to ask after your health.

HELEN. *(Abstractedly)* Has it been so long, Mr. Throstle? Forgive me, I thank you.

THROSTLE. *(To PETER)* I trust, sir, that your first impressions of England have been confirmed by your—rides about our countryside?

PETER. *(Speaks quite pleasantly)* I love England, sir. (LADY ANNE *and* TOM *watch* PETER *and* THROSTLE.)

THROSTLE. Such an unequivocal declaration warms one's heart. Some men are more backward in confessing their affections.

LADY ANNE. *(Hastily, coming to him* C. *With forced lightness, takes him above settee to door* L.) Dear Mr. Throstle, now do come into the drawing-room and tell me all the gossip. I always count on you for that! (THROSTLE *bows to* HELEN *and* PETER, *turns with* LADY ANNE L., TOM *remaining by fireplace.*)

THROSTLE. *(As he walks* L. *with* LADY ANNE. *Sarcastically)* All the gossip that I hear, ma'am, seems confined to one topic.

LADY ANNE. *(As they go out* L.) I've not stirred from the house these three days. *(Exeunt* LADY ANNE *and* THROSTLE L. PETER *walks to* C. TOM *advances* L.C. *as* HELEN *goes to window up* R. TOM *then walks to* L., *turns at door, looks from* PETER *to* HELEN, *laughs and makes a derisive grimace about* THROSTLE; *he then exits* L. PETER *comes down stage* R.C.)

HELEN. *(By small table* L.C.) Peter, we don't really care about what they say.

PETER. Of course we're always together, and Lady Anne keeps expecting me to say something—

HELEN. *(Walks to him* R.C. *in front. A little strained)* You *are* happy with me, Peter?

*cut to 92*

*all cut*

PETER. *(Embracing her)* Divinely happy! This morning, in those enchanted Richmond woods——

HELEN. The sun on the red leaves!

PETER. Helen, dearest, forgive me. I don't want to drag in everyday, practical things into this dreamland we've been living in——

HELEN. *(Pleadingly)* Then don't, Peter! *(Turns, walks to window R., looking out. Turns as she speaks)* Come out into the Square. We mustn't lose even the twilight of this day that was made just for us!

PETER. *(Still R.C. down stage)* That Throstle—they're *all* talking about us, now! *(Moves up toward HELEN, then to back of settee and toward door L.; turns toward her)* We can't go on like this. Why did you make me promise not to tell them we love each other?

HELEN. You try to keep away from them all. And they know you do, Peter. *(She comes to R. of table C. from window.)*

PETER. Of course I try to keep away from them—to be with you. That's natural, isn't it?

HELEN. When you do have to talk to them you say things you shouldn't. *(She crosses to down C. and to below settee)* Sometimes I'm afraid you'll even tell them—tell them the truth. *(Sits on settee.)*

PETER. *(Crosses down L. and to front of settee)* Oh, Helen, don't bring back the thoughts that are a nightmare! Do you think I'm going out of my head? *(With laugh, sits L. of HELEN)* If I did tell them, it would certainly send *them* out of theirs.

HELEN. *(Sadly)* Can't you think of it as I do, as a fairy story, and not as a nightmare? Don't you see the difference? They're both impossible, but fairy stories are beautiful and nightmares are ugly.

PETER. What is the end of every fairy tale?

HELEN. *(Murmurs, looking at him)* And so they lived happily ever afterwards.

PETER. Then make this a *true* fairy story! Let me go to Lady Anne!

HELEN. How can I when, even though you love me, your mind and body ache to get back?

PETER. *(Sits back)* They don't, Helen, they don't; I adore the peace of old things, the quiet and the charm——

HELEN. You don't deceive me. 'Tis true that you were fond of what's left in your world of our poor little London that is here now. But I feel the loathing and contempt in your heart, and the fear! Your whole soul yearns for your own life.

PETER. *(This almost kills* PETER'S *ease and happiness for a moment, but he quickly throws off any depression)* Helen, how can it matter to me where I am or what world I'm in, if I have you with me?

HELEN. You're like an angel who should put off his wings and give up his heaven to live on earth with a girl who loves him.

PETER. Heaven! I thought of it when I lived in it as all raw nerves and clatter and ugliness.

HELEN. But you don't think that now as you look back on it, Peter. Oh, I've watched you, and you've let things slip. When you were talking of the thrill of speed you said we all live here with chains on our feet—and you said, if I thought your city was Paradise by day, I ought to see it in the winter evenings, when the lights come on—and even in the woods at Richmond you said you wished you had a cigarette! *(A slight smile at him.)*

PETER. Oh, curse cigarettes! Give me yourself and I can forget it all and be happy in our love.

HELEN. *(Suddenly, taking his hand)* Peter, did you sleep last night?

*(WARN Hoofs and Coach.)*

PETER. *(Leans back in seat—speaks lightly)* Do people really *sleep,* in the eighteenth century?

HELEN. *(Distressed)* Oh, my love, I knew it!

PETER. Why, that's nothing at all, Helen. I shall be all right when I really have *you!*

HELEN. *(Sadly, doubtfully, murmurs—turns away)* When you have me.

PETER. My darling—the way you say that, as though it would never happen!—you make me afraid —tell me that you never think of this as a love of ghost for ghost! Even though you love me so, don't you think of me sometimes as a phantom who hasn't been born yet, as a shadow?

HELEN. *(Kisses him passionately)* Dear shadow!

PETER. Your kisses! You seem all spirit and white fire, not flesh and blood at all, excepting when you kiss me, and then I know that you want me as I want you, and that whatever else of terror and mystery there may be, our love is the old everlasting love of man and girl——

HELEN. Something more! *(Rises; turns from him)* Perhaps something less!

PETER. *(Rises)* Not something less! We're going to live out our lives here together! *(HOOFS and COACH heard off.)*

HELEN. *(Turns to him; embraces him)* I want to believe it, Peter! Make me believe it!

PETER. I will, Helen; I can and I will! *(Starts a step* L.*)* I'll go to Lady Anne right away. *(Comes back to her)* That's what I need: to feel that I've taken the plunge, that it's settled! And you want me, you need me too! Why else has this wonder happened? *(Door opens* L. *They disengage.* TOM *enters; looks from one to the other uneasily.)*

TOM. Too occupied to hear it, I suppose?

PETER. What do you mean?

TOM. Oh, a coach has stopped at the door. *(Walking to window* R., *back of them. Turns; walks* C. *front)* Someone has got out, that's all.

HELEN. Kate!

TOM. *(Chaffingly)* Gad, a fellow can't tell **you**

two anything you don't already know! I wish I had second sight! *(Seriously)* Better go in there and let me talk to her. She'll need a little preparation, eh, cousin? (PETER *and* HELEN *look at one another.* HELEN *motions toward door* L. HELEN *and* PETER *go out together.* TOM *strolls to mirror, adjusts cravat, humming, "Let schoolmasters puzzle their brains." Enter* KATE R. *in hat and traveling costume. She puts hat in chair by door* R.; *walks* R. *front.* TOM *meets her.* TOM, *affecting surprise)* Gad's life! You! Better be scared to death in town than bored to death in the country, eh, sister? You'd never believe the luck I've had at White's the week you've been at Budleigh!

KATE. *(Cold, suppressed emotion)* I know what has happened.

TOM. Oh, indeed? News travels fast, it seems. You've not developed second sight, too, by any chance?

KATE. *(A step toward him)* Where is Mr. Standish?

TOM. *Mr.* Standish, is it now? Now look'ee, sister! I'd blame no woman for not having our Yankee mystery-monger. But, thank God, for all our sakes, there's someone who doesn't feel as you do, and now you're back, you *must* be civil to him.

KATE. Where is he?

TOM. *(Turns; walks toward window* L. KATE *puts gloves on table* R. *of settee)* He's where and with whom he should be. *(Looks out of window and exclaims with surprise)* Gad's life, now the cat's come home the mice have scampered off! So, he opens the gate! The fountain plays in the Square! *(Mimicking* DUKE*)* "A fine bair ov lofers!" (KATE *goes to window* R., *looks, turns, covers her face with hands)* Eh, what's wrong with you?

KATE. This shall never be.

TOM. *(Angrily)* Who says so?

KATE. I say so!

TOM. Hell and damnation! First you put aside the settlement and ten thousand a year yourself; now, a week later, you post to town to stop Helen from bringing it into the family! (KATE *crosses him* L., *tugs bell-pull sharply. He follows her*) Now, Kate, no mischief. 'Tis no more your affair.

KATE. (*Comes behind* L. *end of settee; he comes behind* R. *end of settee*) I'd rather see Helen in her coffin than the wife of Peter Standish!

TOM. 'Slife, if you set her against him!

KATE. So, because you've had his money and can't pay if we break with him, you'd see your sister damned!

TOM. (*Furious, but confused*) See my sister damned! You're my sister, and I say damn you— for not minding your own business. (*Enter* MAID R. TOM *walks* L. *up stage.*)

KATE. (*With a gesture to window*) Mr. Standish is walking in the Square with Miss Helen. Ask him to come here to me. Wilk ons

MAID. Yes, madam. (*Exits* R.)

TOM. (*With ugly laugh, walks back to former position behind settee*) We'll see what Mother has to say to your pretty scheme!

KATE. (*Crosses* D.C.) You think you're but selling Helen for money, as girls are sold every day.

TOM. Sell, indeed! The girl dotes on him!

KATE. Then she's bewitched, as I was!

TOM. As you *are,* you mean! There's to be no meddling, you hear me, no meddling!

LADY ANNE. (*Enters* L., *followed by* THROSTLE) Thomas! (*Comes behind settee to* R. *of it.* TOM *falling back* R.C. *Surprise*) What, Kate, you here! (KATE *curtseys.* THROSTLE *bows.* THROSTLE *stands in front of* L. *end of settee, facing* KATE. LADY ANNE *turns to* THROSTLE, *expecting him to take his leave*) Mr. Throstle——

KATE. *(Crosses to* L. *end of settee)* Mr. Throstle, don't go—help me to save her! (KATE *sits on* L. *end of settee.* THROSTLE *bows and stays.)*

LADY ANNE. *(Angrily, to* KATE, *crosses* D.C.) What, have you not repented of your folly?

TOM. *(Speaks to* LADY ANNE, *on her* R.) No, and she would commit worse folly. Won't have Peter herself, and now has him fetched here to tell him he shan't have Helen.

LADY ANNE. *(Turning to* THROSTLE) Dear sir, pray return to us when we are not in turmoil. (THROSTLE *bows uncertainly.)*

TOM. *(Suspiciously, to* KATE) Where did you hear all this?

KATE. *(Facing* THROSTLE) Oh, Mr. Throstle, *you* understand—stay and help me!

THROSTLE. Madam, is ten thousand a year worth the loss of Miss Helen's happiness?

LADY ANNE. *(Moves up in front,* R. *end of settee)* Eh, what's this, Mr. Throstle? Who speaks of loss of happiness?

TOM. *(To* LADY ANNE) He's a party to this; he's been writing to her about Helen!

LADY ANNE. Is this true, Mr. Throstle?

THROSTLE. *(Standing down* L.) Madam, Mr. Standish is no fit mate for any mortal woman.

KATE. You *know,* you *know!*

THROSTLE. God will not permit it.

LADY ANNE. What treachery is this, Mr. Throstle?

KATE. *(Crying)* I must open your eyes, ma'am. I came back to save her, and she's out there now— *(Gesture to window)*—with *that!* Oh, my poor sister!

TOM. *(In half whisper)* Throstle is concerned in this, ma'am. Be high with her, pack her off again, or she'll bedevil everything. (THROSTLE *moves up to window* L.)

LADY ANNE. Be calm, Thomas. This is in *my*

hands. *(Advancing toward* KATE*)* Kate, if you cannot master this strange perversity, you must return to Budleigh. *(Turns to* THROSTLE*)* Sir, I beg you to carry your plots and stratagems elsewhere. *(*THROSTLE *bows; walks* L. *toward doors* L. LADY ANNE *turns to* TOM *with attitude of "I run my family.")*

KATE. *(After slight pause)* This marriage must not be!

LADY ANNE. *(Step* L. *toward* KATE*)* What, hussy—"must not be"?

TOM. Now you see, ma'am! *(Crosses up* R.; *sits before desk.)*

LADY ANNE. *(Walks up to* KATE *with dignity to before* R. *end of settee; looks her in the eyes)* You will beg my pardon, miss, for this unheard-of insolence.

KATE. *(Stands her ground)* I told you I'd not have him, did I not love him? I did love him; he cast his spell on me, but God took pity and saved me.

LADY ANNE. More of this and I will have physicians to you.

PETER. *(Enters from* R. *and crosses to* R.C.*)* I'm glad you've come back, Kate—— *(Sees others and hesitates)* Everybody seems to have turned out to welcome you home.

KATE. *(Crosses to* L. *of him)* Mr. Standish! When you came into this house, though the door was shut and locked, *did* you come from America?

LADY ANNE. *(Turning on her, furiously)* To your room! To your room, I say!

KATE. *(To* LADY ANNE*)* I remain till I've had my answer. *(To* PETER*)* Sir, do you *really* come from America? *(*LADY ANNE *walks to* L. *end of settee.* THROSTLE *turns from window* R. *to down* R., *below* TOM.*)*

PETER. I do. That's true. But, Kate—— *(He

"Berkeley Square"                    Act III, See Page 101

*tries to bring up the subject of* HELEN, *but* KATE *interrupts.*)

KATE. (C. *Cold, determined force*) I made a list of ten of his phrases. He said they were used in New York. On my way home I stopped at the Legation in Grosvenor Square. Should not the American Minister, Mr. Adams, know what words are used in New York?

PETER. (R.C.) He's from Massachusetts.

KATE. I asked him. He had never heard one of the ten! So you see, those words are not used in America! They are not used in England! They are not used in this world! (*Violently. Backs up* C.) The devils use them, in hell!

TOM. (*Rises*) Hark'ee, Kate, you mad wench! That Throstle skulking over there, who is as mad as you now, spoke to Mr. Adams, and the Yankee Minister knew Peter in New York.

KATE. Peter Standish came from New York in the *General Wolfe*—his body stands there—(*To* PETER)—but what have you done with *him?*

LADY ANNE. Poor abused cousin! (*Crossing to* L. *of* KATE, *via above settee.*)

KATE. (*Turns on her*) In the old days he'd have been burned, he'd have been burned at the stake! (THROSTLE *walks few steps down* R.C., *behind* PETER. PETER *has gradually turned his back to audience—is standing down* C., *facing up stage.*)

PETER. Why not now? You burn people still—you burn women!

LADY ANNE. (*Up*) Physicians, restraint, *confinement! Straps!*

TOM. I'll drag her upstairs, ma'am. (*Starts for* KATE *via above* PETER, *who stops him.*)

PETER. (*Suddenly beside himself, stopping* TOM) Yes, *and whips!* Whip her, if she's crazy, flog her in public, as you flog your half-naked lunatics at

Bedlam, with a crowd of your gaping Londoners looking on—you savages!

KATE. *(Standing up* L.C. LADY ANNE L. *of her)* You have stolen his body, but what have you done with his *soul?*

PETER. *(Laughing hysterically)* "His soul goes marching on! John Brown's body lies a-mouldering in the grave." *(During this* PETER *advances on* THROSTLE *with wild gesture. He retreats a step to down* R. *He finishes "mouldering in his grave" looking up* C. *at* TOM, *who is* R. *of* KATE—*at* KATE, *who is* L.C., *and* LADY ANNE, *who is* L. *of* KATE.)

TOM. *(Comes a step down* C.) She's out of her head. Never mind what she thinks about you!

PETER. *(To* TOM, *turning on him quickly* C.) And what do *you* think about me? *(*TOM *retreats two steps up* C., *averting eyes, and retreats a few steps more,* PETER *moving up to him, during following)* You daren't look me in the eyes, yet you'd marry me to your sister. D'you think I don't know why? You—a gentleman! Insolence, ignorance and dirt! Making a beast of yourself with drink and debauching servant girls! And you're no worse than your Prince—you are a typical English gentleman of your time—God! What a time! *(Crosses a step down* R.C.)

THROSTLE. *(To* PETER) Sir, a gentleman of New York——

PETER. *(Turns on* THROSTLE, *who has come a step toward* PETER. THROSTLE *stands his ground for a time, but finally backs up)* You and your friends know it all, don't they, Throstle? So you despise your rude barbarian forbears, do you? Well, we who know better, love them and despise you! No warmth in your blood, no soul in your art! A new fire of London, that's what's needed here; yes, and a new plague, too! Dirt, disease, cruelty, smells! *(Turning on* KATE, *taking a few steps* L.) You,

Kate, you may be a fool, but you're the best of the lot, for you're trying in your silly way to help Helen now, and I love you for it! *(Advances toward* LADY ANNE, *coming to* R. *of small table, while* LADY ANNE, *standing behind settee, retreats* L. *beyond settee.* TOM *crosses down* R. *to* THROSTLE.*)* Madam, I've seen you in Sheridan's plays; I've read you in Jane Austen's novels. You know what you want, and you plough straight ahead over everything, through everything, like a tank, lumbering through the mud! *(Laughs wildly, turning on* KATE, *talking to her across small table as she stands* L. *behind settee)* You hear that, Kate! Like a tank! Go to the American Legation and ask Charles Francis Adams what "tank" means! No, it's not Charles Francis Adams who's minister here now, it's his grandfather, John Adams, second President of the United States. Charles Francis Adams isn't born yet; he won't be born until the Civil War in 1861. What's one blunder among so many? Peter Standish came from New York to Plymouth in the *General Wolfe,* did he? *(Advancing down* C.*)* Peter Standish came from New York to Plymouth in the *Mauretania!* *(Pauses, looks around at them, almost gibbering, to see how they take this)* Shall I make a few more blunders for you to gibber at? *(Takes two steps toward* KATE, *who retreats a little)* Shall I drive you back to Budleigh in my car, fifty miles an hour? No, not on a broomstick! *(Turns, comes behind small table again, shouting at* LADY ANNE*)* Shall I sell that portrait for you in America, madam, for thirty thousand pounds? *(Half turns, shaking right arm at tapestry panel, shouts as he turns and rushes up to tapestry)* The Americans buy all the Reynoldses! *(Stops dead, arms outstretched, gazing at tapestry. The others exchange glances.* TOM *shrugs shoulders.* LADY ANNE *steps forward as though to go to him when he turns. Continues, shrinking back*

*against console table)* What do I care about you?
(KATE *edges to* R. *end of fireplace.)* You're all over
and done with! *(Sidles along rear wall* L., *afraid,
grasping curtain of window for support)* You're all
dead—you've all rotted in your graves—you're all
ghosts, that's what you are—ghosts! (KATE *turns
quickly; exits* L., *followed by* LADY ANNE.)

TOM. *(Runs across stage from* R. *to* L. *and exits)*
God, she's going to Helen! (PETER *stares after
them.)*

THROSTLE. *(Who has been standing in front of
desk, comes forward* R.C.) Sir, a word with you!
(PETER *at window* L., *turns to him.)* You have won
her affections, as you could win those of any woman
who did not fear you.

PETER. *(Feverishly, walking toward him up* C.)
What the devil do you mean?

THROSTLE. Sir, you do not even intend to make
her your wife?

PETER. *(Beside himself)* You dead and buried
little pip-squeak—— *(Advancing on* THROSTLE, *who
hastily turns, seizes candlesticks from desk.)* You
dare to soil with your dirty mind——

THROSTLE. *(Turns in front of desk as* PETER *is
about to strike him, holding candlesticks in the form
of the Cross)* Retro me, Sathanas.

THROSTLE. Adjuro ergo
te, draco nequissime, in
nomine agni immaculati.
Adjuro ergo te, omnis im-
mundissime spiritus, omne
phantasma, omnis incursio
satanae.

PETER. *(Stops, whip
poised in midair, laughs
hysterically; slings whip
across room)* Ha! Exor-
cism! Throstle casts out
the devil! Banned by bell,
book and candle! You've
got *two* candles, but
where's your book,
where's your bell? Most
irregular! *(P a u s e s.*

Exi ergo, impius, exi sce-
lerate, exi cum omni fal-

THROSTLE'S *phrases are*

| | |
|---|---|
| lacia tua, quia hominum | heard alone for a mo- |
| templum suum esse voluit | ment. *More violently)* |
| Deus—— | So you send me back to |
| | hell where I came from, |
| | do you? I'm to vanish in |
| | a clap of thunder, am I? |
| | *(Stands on toes, fingers* |
| | *crooked, towering over* |
| | THROSTLE *like Mephisto)* |
| | Smell the brimstone, |
| | Throstle. Can't you |
| Exi ergo, transgressor. | smell the brimstone? |
| Exi seductor, plene omnis | Shall I take off my shoe |
| doli et fallaciae, virtutis | and show you the cloven |
| inimicus,       innocentium | hoof? I'll set ten devils |
| prosecutor! | on you, damn your soul! |

*(During latter part of scene,* THROSTLE *has re-treated few steps toward door* R. *He is in front of chair, between door and desk, when* PETER *wrenches away candlesticks, throws them to floor behind settee.* THROSTLE, *with a hoarse scream, but still facing* PETER, *pulls door open, exits* R.)

PETER. *(Turns, walks few steps almost to small table, then, head in hand, turns up and staggers to window* R., *grasping curtain with left hand and looking out in pose he adopts at curtain in the first act. After pause. Quietly, voice shaking)* And I was in love with the past! *(Turns, walks diagonally to settee as he says)* Is that a crime? Is it as bad as murder? It must be, for see what my sentence is—— *(Passing around in front of small table to settee)* Imprisonment for life, for life, for life—— *(Sinks on settee,* R. *end; buries head in hands, elbows resting on small table)* —in this filthy little pigsty of a world! *(Collapses, head in hands, on table.)*

HELEN. *(After pause, enter* HELEN L. *She sees* PETER's *back; comes front to* L. *side of settee; stops)* Peter! Is it you? *(He rises, back to her)* Say you are not the other! *(*PETER *turns to her. She runs to him. They embrace before settee.)* I was afraid *he* had come.

PETER. He isn't here. He can't be. It takes us both to do it! *(Reproachfully)* So you thought I might have *sneaked* back!

HELEN. No, no!

PETER. Then you've heard. You thought I'd do it while I was out of my head. Even if I *were* mad, I'd never leave you! I told them it's for life—for life! *(She releases herself from him and steps back slightly)* Let him stay there and be damned. I've made my choice. *(*PETER *standing before small table,* HELEN *before settee.)*

HELEN. *(Appealingly)* 'Tis beyond your strength.

PETER. You do not know my strength. Oh, Helen, Kate *knows,* and Throstle——

HELEN. I know, Peter, they baited you. You told them how you hate their world, my world——

PETER. *(Takes her hands)* I was blaspheming, since you are part of it.

HELEN. You told them how you feel buried alive —among the dead. *(*PETER *buries head in hands.)* And now, you can never see them again.

PETER. *(Standing before settee)* We'll go away together! To America!

HELEN. People would hate and fear you, anywhere.

PETER. Why should they hate me?

HELEN. They hate what they fear, just as you fear and hate them, my changeling.

PETER. I can face them all, for you belong to me, not them. *(Starts to kiss her.)*

HELEN. *(Gently repulses him)* I'm strong now. Don't make me weak again! *(Sinks on* L. *end of settee. He stands, back to audience)* Each night I've said, "He must go back!" But each morning, when we'd ride away together, I'd think, "Let me have only one more day!"

PETER. No, we're going to tell them—— *(Sits by her)* You agreed, Helen!

HELEN. *(Finality in tone)* My darling, I've known that you must go. Except when to be with you made me a coward again, when I let you convince me, only because I *wanted* to be convinced. But *after this*——

PETER. Don't, Helen! I was a fool, a weakling. It won't happen again. I couldn't face my own life without you.

HELEN. What life is this for you? Be brave, Peter, and listen! My life, my London, are nightmares to you. (PETER's *head drops.*) No sad thoughts now, my Peter. We two alone have been chosen for this wonder out of all the millions of lovers since time began. Our love is against nature, you said, and so it can't be real; but it *is* real, more real, Peter, than if you had been born in my world, or I in yours, because—it is a miracle. Think of what has been given us, not of what is taken away!

PETER. Nothing can be taken away; that we have come together at all, doesn't that prove that we weren't meant to lose each other?

HELEN. Yes, yes, and we shall be together always, Peter—not in my time, nor in yours, but in God's.

PETER. Yes, but Helen, I want you *now*—this is our one life on earth!

HELEN. *Our* life on earth? Oh, Peter, think more clearly!

PETER. *(Turns to her)* You can't want me to go back! You love me!

HELEN. With all my soul.

PETER. Then I stay here!

HELEN. *(Rises)* Stay, then, Peter! "For life—for life"—a life of nightmare that never ends! So that I may watch you in torment, when I cannot help you! So that you may live on in my world, in a living death, *mad! (Comes to him; kneels beside him)* Because you love me, you condemn me to *that?* (PETER *buries his face on her* R. *shoulder.)* You *do* see it! Leave me, while our love is still beautiful! I ask it for *my* sake. *(RUMBLE of thunder. She rises. Pause.* PETER *rises; turns slowly; takes a few mechanical steps toward the panel where the picture hangs in 1928. He stops, then goes up to console table, extends his hands to the panel, in gesture of surrender.* HELEN *still stands* L. *of settee, not looking at him. RUMBLE stops.)*

PETER. *(Turns; crosses a step or two down* C.) But now *he* will be here, in my place, with my body! *(Few steps down stage)* How can *you* bear *that?*

*(WARN Clock.)*

HELEN. *(Not looking at him)* Love will give me strength. *(Turns away, head in hands, as he walks slowly down* C. *front, looking out. She speaks half over her shoulder; they cannot look at one another)* You've your life to live out in the future, Peter. Don't be too sad there about a girl who's been dead so long. *(Turns to face him)* As I grow old, your youth will seem to me eternal youth, for you *will* come, won't you, young as I see you now, to my grave in St. Mark's churchyard? To you, that will be tomorrow. And yet, 'twill be generations after I am dead. I'll ask for a stone with the letters cut deep, so they won't wear away, before you come to me. And you must come—alone.

PETER. Alone? *(He stands* C. *front. She is in front of Left side of settee.)*

HELEN. *(Turns away from him again)* But if you love that girl, you must marry her.

PETER. Don't, don't!

HELEN. *(Turns to him again)* You *can't* live in this house with only that old woman to look after you. When that happens I shall be—— And yet, I *am* jealous, even though I *will* be dead.

PETER. I love you only, now and in my own time and in whatever other times may come. (HELEN *takes three steps toward him, coming to just beyond small table.*)

HELEN. I believe. Forgive me. *(The afternoon light has been gradually dimming. CLOCK on landing strikes once. They both start; he steps back, two steps; stops as* HELEN *speaks)* If only you could take back with you just one thing that was mine! *(Turns, opens* L. *hand drawer in small table* L.C.; *takes out Crux Ansata)* Father got this in Egypt, while the fleet was there. In some strange way it has meant so much to me. (PETER *looks up slowly.*)

PETER. *(Overwhelmed)* The Crux Ansata!

HELEN. *(During this they are separated by four feet)* What is it?

PETER. The symbol of Life, and of Eternity!

HELEN. Then that's why I loved it so.

PETER. Helen! This was mine—long ago!

HELEN. *(Uncomprehending)* Yours—long ago?

PETER. *(Points)* It was standing over there, when I first entered this room—in the Future. *(It has now grown DUSK.)*

HELEN. This little thing—has crossed the great darkness between us. Mine while I live, yours in the world that I shall never see. (PETER *steps toward her; she holds out the Crux Ansata in her* R. *hand as though to ward him off, and takes step backward) This* was our parting! (PETER *walks backward toward door* R., *slowly and mechanically. Door* R. *opens as he is four feet away from it.* LADY ANNE *enters, stops and exclaims violently on seeing* PETER. *She is terrified, and for the first time.* HELEN *remains motionless.)*

LADY ANNE. Eh—what—*you here!* I saw you as I came up, drinking with Tom in the study! How, then, are you here before me?

PETER. *(Slowly as in a trance—still looking at* HELEN*)* I passed you on the stairs as you turned your head.

LADY ANNE. *(Accepting his explanation)* I vow you run like a cat. (PETER *backs out* R*., as* LADY ANNE *is crossing to above settee and picking up candlesticks.* PETER *closes door as she puts them on the table. She closes drawer in table which* HELEN *left open; comes around* L*. of settee; sits.* HELEN *still motionless.)* Why have you brought out that ugly old Egyptian thing?

HELEN. *(Walks up stage to* L*. of window* R*., turns, holds Crux Ansata in front of her against her breast and looks fixedly out front)* No more, dear shadows! (LADY ANNE *glances at* HELEN.)

LADY ANNE. Frenzy from them, moonshine from you! He seemed quiet. Are his wits then restored? *(Pause.* HELEN *standing looking fixedly before her.)* Are you not well, child? *(Pause, which lasts for count of five.* TOM *enters* R*.; looks from one to the other importantly. Stops near door.)*

TOM. Gad's life, what an afternoon! Two lunatics in one house are too many for any man's stomach. God knows what devilment Kate will concoct when she's up to it again, but I've one piece of good news for you he's just been telling me in the study, poor devil. He's been ill, ever since he came here. *(Tapping forehead)* Can't remember a thing that's happened. Didn't even remember me. Gaped at me and said, "Mr. Pettigrew, I presume?"

LADY ANNE. *(Up and comes* C*. front.* TOM *meets her* C*.)* Oh, then his wits must be quite, quite gone!

TOM. But no, ma'am; they've come back! He's cured! That frenzy in here was but the end of a fever. 'Twas only the fever made his brain work oddly, so that everyone feared him—he's like one of us now. *(Pauses, turns to audience, puzzled)* That's it—*one of us!*

LADY ANNE. *(Relieved)* Ah! And now may God's mercy remember Kate as well! *(Comes L. to doors—via below settee)* I said all along 'twas superstitious gabble. *(As she goes out L.)* A fever, poor dear man! *(Exits L.)*

TOM. I never could make the fellow swallow above half a bottle. And now he's laid me five guineas— *(Turns to door R.)*—he'll drink me under the table! *(Looks out door R.)* Here he comes upstairs!

HELEN. *(Coming down stage C. to level with door R.)* Leave *me* alone with him!

TOM. *You!* 'Tis Kate he wants to see! *(Exits R., closing door, calling in boisterous chaff)* You Yankee mystery-monger!

HELEN. *(Repeats mechanically as she places cross on table down C.)* One of us—now! *(The doorknob R. turns. The door opens slowly. HELEN turns to door; curtseys slowly as the CURTAIN falls.)*

## SLOW CURTAIN

## SCENE TWO

SCENE: *The curtain rises in 1928 at the relative moment when it fell on the preceding scene in 1784. Scene set as in Act I, Scene II. Portrait hangs as before. Curtains closed. One candle burning on desk; two on small table between couch and armchair. No other lights, excepting from the fire. Light switch hangs from wall to* L. *of door* R. *by torn wires. Crux Ansata on writing-table.*

MARJORIE *and* AMBASSADOR *are shown in* R. *by* MRS. BARWICK, *who is talking volubly as she enters.* MRS. BARWICK *stops near door* R. *as she talks.* AMBASSADOR *stops* R.C. MARJORIE *crosses to small table, puts hat on it, then continues to* L., *then up* L.; *sees picture; looks at it; crosses a step to it.*

MRS. BARWICK. —but it wasn't anything definite he said, Miss; it was the tone of his voice and the way he looked at me when he was going out, sir, as though he was seeing the last of me. That was why I took the liberty of telephoning the Embassy, your Excellency.

AMBASSADOR. *(Interrupting)* Quite right, too, Mrs. Barwick, even if it turns out a false alarm. You've had the patience of Job, and nobody will appreciate it so much as Mr. Standish when he's well again. But why are you using candles all over the house? Can't we talk this over better if we have some real light? (MARJORIE *crosses from* L. *a step or two.)*

MRS. BARWICK. It's no good, your Excellency, the lights aren't working.

MARJORIE. *(Impatiently. Crosses down to* L. *of couch)* Oh, dear, what does that matter?

MRS. BARWICK. He did it himself, sir; he tore out this fitting last night—*(Handles broken and dangling light switch)* —then he smashed the main switchboard downstairs.

AMBASSADOR. *(Crossing toward* MARJORIE*)* But when this thing first came on him he was *fascinated* by the light. *(To* MRS. BARWICK*)* Kept turning it on and off.

MARJORIE. *(Faces him)* Oh, Mr. Ambassador, we didn't come here to talk about electric light! We've got to find him right away before anything can happen to him.

AMBASSADOR. There, there, my dear, I'm sure he's all right, wherever he is.

MARJORIE. Now pull yourself together, Mrs. Barwick—(AMBASSADOR *sits in armchair*)—and try and be clear and definite. How long has he been gone?

MRS. BARWICK. *(Crosses a step* C.*)* I heard the clock strike the quarter, Miss, as he went downstairs and out the front door.

MARJORIE. *(To* AMBASSADOR. *Sits on, settee)* This is terrible; it was wicked to leave him alone here when he was so ill; we ought to have sent him where he can be taken care of.

AMBASSADOR. *(Leaning on table toward her)* My dear, I've been in touch with Sir William Briggs all along, but Peter has been one too many for us. He won't give himself away to the doctors——

MARJORIE. Won't give himself away! Why, those drunken scrapes, when he shouts old curses and drinking songs, his gambling and scattering I O U's all over London, telling people that he's ten thousand pounds a year but some other man has got hold of all his money—*surely,* any doctor with a grain of sense——

AMBASSADOR. Ah, no, Marjorie, of course we who know Peter—but to convince others there must be some definite symptoms.

MARJORIE. *(Rising—moves Left)* Anyway, we've got to find him now; we must follow him!

AMBASSADOR. But we haven't anything to go on yet. *(She stands at L. end of settee—cries—attitude of complete misery.)* You mustn't be so upset, Marjorie. Of course he'll come back. Where could he go? And he didn't even say he wasn't coming back. Now, Mrs. Barwick, has anything in particular happened since I was here?

MRS. BARWICK. Well, sir, some people came from a night club. He was shouting at them, sir. I—I listened, sir. I thought it my duty, sir, so I could tell you, sir.

AMBASSADOR. Oh, quite right, Mrs. Barwick.

MRS. BARWICK. He yelled at them, sir. He said they weren't alive and they wouldn't be born for another hundred years. And when they laughed at him he hit one of them and then they went away and I found him drunk on the floor, Miss. *(Cries.)*

---

*(Door R. opens slowly. PETER comes in carrying a sheet of paper. He wears a lounge suit. He looks pale and dazed and, without seeing the others, lays the paper down on writing-bureau, placing the Crux Ansata on it. As he enters, MARJORIE and AMBASSADOR rise. AMBASSADOR clears throat.)*

PETER. *(Turns; comes R. front between MRS. BARWICK and AMBASSADOR)* Mr. Ambassador!

AMBASSADOR. I just thought I'd look in, Peter.

I've taken the liberty of bringing a great friend of mine—— *(Crosses up* C.*)*

PETER. *(Goes toward settee)* Marjorie!

MARJORIE. *(Steps toward him)* Peter! You know me! *(Holds up her face for him to kiss.* PETER *crosses to her; he takes her hands and kisses them as in the fashion of the Eighteenth Century.)*

PETER. Of course. *(Turning to* MRS. BARWICK, *who has moved to go out* R.*)* Mrs. Barwick, I'm afraid—Peter Standish—has been giving you a lot of trouble.

MRS. BARWICK. *(Delighted)* Oh, sir, it's all right now! *(She goes out* L. *almost joyfully, closing the door.* AMBASSADOR *crosses down stage, looking at* PETER.*)*

PETER. *(Turns to* AMBASSADOR, *who is* R. *front)* So you think I'm still the other man?

AMBASSADOR. *(Looks at portrait, back again to* PETER*)* I'm blessed if I know what I think.

MARJORIE. *(Overjoyed)* It's all right *now,* Mr. Ambassador!

PETER. Mr. Ambassador, all my thanks for your kindness! If you'll forgive me, I must talk to Marjorie now.

AMBASSADOR. *(Disturbed)* Don't you think perhaps——

PETER. You may take it that I'm myself again.

AMBASSADOR. Very well! *(Moves toward desk.)*

MARJORIE. *(Runs after him, crossing* PETER, *who turns away and stands by armchair)* Mr. Ambassador! *(They are* R.C.*)* Please go. You understand.

AMBASSADOR. *(Reluctantly to* MARJORIE*)* I'll wait downstairs——

MARJORIE. Thank you. *(Exit* AMBASSADOR R., *leaving door slightly ajar.* MARJORIE *watches him off, turning at* R.C. *and watching* PETER.*)*

PETER. *(A pause. Slowly turns;* MARJORIE *stands*

R.C.*)* We were going to be married. It seems so very long ago.

MARJORIE. *(Happily—speaks softly—crosses a step or two to him)* You remember!

PETER. *(His head turns toward portrait)* The Ambassador came here and found——

MARJORIE. He found my poor Peter ill, but now he's cured.

PETER. *(Walks to portrait, back to her)* I'm incurable.

MARJORIE. You *are* cured. If you remember me, you can't think any longer that—*(Gesture to portrait)*—you're—*him.*

PETER. *(Distressed)* You couldn't marry me after this, could you?

MARJORIE. Never mind that now, Peter. I'm here to take care of you.

PETER. *(Walks slowly up to her R.C. as he speaks, walking in front of armchair)* Marjorie! Something has happened, something you could never believe. *(Turns away)* And now I must live here—*(Turns back to her)*—alone. (R. of table L.C.)

MARJORIE. *(After a pause, turns away, her voice shaking)* In this house, with only your old woman? Why, the place can't even be kept clean.

PETER. I'll shut up most of it. *(Travels on a few steps.)*

MARJORIE. *(Taking charge of him a bit)* Peter, you know, you can't afford it.

PETER. *(In front of couch)* No—but I'll keep this room—*(As though to himself)* —just as it was, *always.* (MARJORIE *remains motionless. He walks around couch to window L., looking out.)*

MARJORIE. *(She sees his distress and begins again in a different voice—facing front)* Never mind, Peter. But I can't break an old habit. I shall go on looking after you, even if it's from a long way off.

PETER. *(Turning)* I feel such a beast.

MARJORIE. *(Sure of herself by now)* You're fine and honest as always, Peter. It's all right. *(Crosses to desk)* Tell me about your work. *(Crosses to writing-bureau)* This Egyptian thing used to be over there. *(She takes the Crux Ansata, walks with it towards console table.* PETER *turns, almost snatches it from her, saying "Please." Comes down to small table; puts it down; sits in armchair, looking at it.* MARJORIE, *astonished and hurt, says, after he sits)* Why, Peter, what's the matter? *(Then turns and ruffles papers on writing-bureau)* Is this the draft for your new architecture book? May I look?

PETER. *(Subconsciously answers her)* Of course.

MARJORIE. *(Picks up paper and looks at it)* Why, here's an epitaph.

PETER. *(Dazed, speaks from now on mechanically, facing away to L., not looking at her)* I copied it, just now, from a tombstone in St. Mark's church-yard.

MARJORIE. *(Coming to him with a paper)* Whose epitaph is it?

PETER. A girl who died one hundred and forty-one years ago.

MARJORIE. Who was she?

PETER. A cousin of Peter Standish. *(*MARJORIE *glances at picture.)*

MARJORIE. *(Looking at paper)* It's Latin. What's it all mean? *(Extends paper to him.* PETER *takes it mechanically, holding it with both hands so that it catches the light from the candles on table.* MAR-JORIE *standing beside the right hand of his chair.* PETER's *head droops.)* Peter! You're crying! Who was that girl who's been dead for ages? Peter, speak to me! *(Turns away; turns again to him)* Don't you know me, Peter? *(Moves toward door R., hesitates, turns to him again. Very softly)* You want me to go? *(He does not answer.* MARJORIE *turns away toward door, hesitates, looks back again at* PETER— *turns and goes slowly out* R., *closing door.)*

PETER. *(Has not moved. After pause, raises paper as before to candlelight)* Hic jacet. "Here lies, in the confident hope of the blessed resurrection, and life eternal, Helen Pettigrew, beloved younger daughter of Sir William Pettigrew, K.B., Vice-Admiral of the Blue, and The Lady Anne Pettigrew, who departed this life June the fifteenth, 1787, aged twenty-three years——" *(His voice breaks down. The paper flutters to the floor.* PETER *remains motionless in the same pose for some moments before the CURTAIN falls slowly.)*

CURTAIN

## "BERKELEY SQUARE"

## PROPERTY PLOT

## ACT I, SCENE I AND III, AND ACT III, SCENE I

1 Half round carpet.
2 Pairs curtains and pelmets.
1 Queen Anne writing-desk (closed).
1 Console table (up center).
1 Console table (dresses off stage L.)
1 Card table (R. of fireplace).
1 Oblong table (3 drawers—R. of settee).
1 Armchair (R. of console table up C.)
1 Wing chair (below doors down L.)
1 Long stool (front of fireplace).
1 Small stool (front of desk).
2 Small straight-backed chairs (1 below fireplace and 1 below writing-desk).
1 Small straight-backed chair (not used as it is broken).
1 Small mirror (on wall between fireplace and doors L.)
1 Bell pull (on wall below mirror).
1 Piece of tapestry (on wall up C.).
1 Settee's cushion.
1 Crux Ansata (in left hand drawer of oblong table in Act III, Scene I, only).
1 Settee (left C.).
2 Candles in two brass candlesticks in Act II through-out and Act III, Scene I.

*OFF STAGE PROPS.*

1 Old newspaper—Act I, Scene I—off R.I. Tom Pettigrew.

1 Taper—Act I, Scene I—off R.I. Maid.

1 Sealed letter—Act I, Scene I—off R.I. Maid.

1 letter opened—Act I, Scene I—off L. Lady Anne.

1 Shawl—Act I, Scene III, off L. Helen Pettigrew.

1 Candle-snuffer.

*HAND PROPS.*

1 Snuffbox—Tom Pettigrew.

1 Snuffbox—Mr. Throstle.

1 Riding-crop—not used.

1 Black leather cigarette case—Peter Standish.

1 Black leather case containing "Miniature"—Peter Standish.

1 Bracelet—Peter Standish.

## ACT II, SCENES I AND II

Same as Act I, Scenes I and II, adding

1 Easel and painting and one Queen Anne armchair to below writing-desk.

and moving

Settee from L.C. to R.C.

Oblong table to L. of settee.

Small stool to below oblong table.

Small straight-backed chair from below fireplace to R.C. of left window and chair from below writing-desk to L.C.

Easel and painting to above writing-desk, facing up stage.

## ACT I, SCENE II, and ACT III, SCENE II

2 Pairs of curtains and 2 pelmets.

1 Armchair (down L. to take place of wing chair in
    this scene).
1 Oil painting (on wall up C. to take place of tap-
    estry which is struck in this scene).
1 Chesterfield settee (L.C. to take place of Queen
    Anne settee which is struck in this scene).
1 Chesterfield armchair (R.C. of settee and R.C. of
    card table which has been moved from right of
    fireplace to R. of settee).
Queen Anne armchair is moved from R. of console
    table to R. of fireplace).
The bowl of flowers from the other scenes is struck
    and a large empty bowl is placed on the console
    table up C. to take its place.
2 Pieces of chelsea on either side of the bowls in all
    scenes.
On the small card table down C. in Act I, Scene II:
    One brass candlestick and candles.
    Box of matches.
In writing desk L. which is now open:
    Crux Ansata both scenes.
    Diary.
    Ashtray.
    Many papers and documents.
    Books.
    In Scene II, Act III, add one lighted candle in a
        brass candlestick.
On small card table down C. in Act III, Scene II:
    Two lighted candles in two brass candlesticks.

*OFF STAGE PROPS.*
    1 Tea set and tray (set for two) off R.—Mrs.
        Barwick.
    1 Glass candlestick and candle—off R.—Mrs. Bar-
        wick.
    1 Old letter—off left—Peter Standish.

*OFF STAGE EFFECTS.*
    1 Rain box.

1 Wind machine.
1 Thunder drum.
1 Set of Chimes.
1 Clock gong.

## ELECTRICAL PLOT

### ELECTRICAL EQUIPMENT, HANGING LIST

First pipe, 14 baby spots, 2 three-lamp section of X-ray.

Back pipe, 5-1000 Watt open hoods (3 blue, 2 frost).

Two 1000-w. open hoods—one under each window up stage.

Tormenter stand with two 2000-w. spots and one 1000-w. spot.

One stand with dimmer—one stand with 1000-w. lamp spot off R.C. entrance (Shadow lamp).

One stand with strip—entrance L.1 (2 amber lamps).

Strip right entrance down in 1. With three amber lamps.

Fire grate.

12 Candle brackets to work off of small dimmer board on battery.

Two wall switches.

One blank wall plate.

One base plug.

One floor plug.

Two table lamps.

One large dimmer box.

Two small dimmer boxes.

One small battery dimmer box.

Eight plugging boxes.

One storage battery.

One battery charger.

Two front lamps in balcony box—ions and cable.

In foots—18 amber—18 blue—9 pink.

## "BERKELEY SQUARE"

## WARDROBE PLOT

## MEN'S COSTUMES

PETER STANDISH: Black dressing-gown, 1 pair black slippers, blue cloth coat, cream breeches, 2 lace handkerchiefs, gray moire coat, breeches, vest, tan cloth coat, top boots, black shoes, 4 jabots, 2 pair spun hose, 2 pair silk hose, 2 wigs.

TOM PETTIGREW: Act I. Green coat and breeches, light waistcoat, lace handkerchief, black shoes, 2 ballet shirts, 2 pair silk hose, 4 ties. Act II: Blue moire coat, white waistcoat, white breeches. Act III: Red riding coat, white breeches, waistcoat, top boots, 2 wigs.

MR. THROSTLE: Act I: Brown brocade costume, 2 ballet shirts, 2 pair hose. Act II: Blue brocade costume, 2 pair black shoes. Act III: Same as Act I. Monocle, 2 wigs.

DUKE OF CUMBERLAND: Act II: Purple velvet costume, diamond star and sash order, 1 wig, 1 lace handkerchief, 2 ballet shirts, 2 pair purple hose, 1 pair black shoes, 2 rings, 1 purple cape with order insignia (made by Eaves).

MAJOR CLINTON: Act II: Red cloth coat, 1 pair white breeches, 2 ballet shirts, 1 pair black shoes, 2 pair white hose, 1 ring of large rhinestones, 1 monocle, 1 wig.

LORD STANLEY: Act II: Black velvet ball costume, sash order and star, black shoes, 2 pair spun hose, 2 ballet shirts, one ring from Miss Mable.

UNDERSTUDY COSTUME: Red velvet ball costume, light waistcoat, black shoes, 2 pair spun hose, 2 ballet shirts.

HELEN PETTIGREW: Act I: Blue silk dress, petticoat, hoop, fan. Act II: Cream satin dress, shoes. Act III: Pink and blue striped dress. Pearl necklace from "Constant Wife." One brooch from the Louis XIV shop, 2 wigs.

KATE PETTIGREW: Act I: Peach taffeta dress, petticoat, hoop, shoes. Act II: Pink taffeta dress, underskirt, fan. Act III: Brown coat and skirt, fancy waistcoat, brown hat, black shoes, gloves, 2 wigs, 2 bracelets.

LADY ANNE PETTIGREW: Act I: Lavender striped dress (Mme. Pous), purple shoes, petticoat, hoop. Act II: Brocade ball dress, fan. Act III: Purple silk dress, underskirt, 2 wigs, 1 amethyst bracelet, Louis IV shop; 1 amethyst ring, Louis XIV shop; 1 brooch, Louis XIV shop; 1 necklace, belonging to production.

MAJOR FRANT: Act I: Three piece tan suit, hat, gloves, purse, shoes. Act III: Dark blue cloth dress, black shoes, 10 large pearl butons, string of large pearls.

DUCHESS OF DEVONSHIRE: Act II: Blue ball dress, 1 pair blue slippers, petticoat, hoop, 1 blue and 1 white feather fan, 1 bracelet paste gold, Louis XIV shop; 1 bowknot brooch and 2 pearl drops, Louis XIV shop; 1 pair bowknot paste earrings, Louis XIV shop; 1 large paste brooch, Miss Mable; 1 wig.

MAID: Act I: Gray dress, cap and apron, 1 pair black shoes, 1 pair white hose. Act II and III, the same as Act I.

MRS. BARWICK: Act I: Gray silk dress, 1 pair shoes, 1 pair hose, 1 wig. Act III: Same as Act I.

MISS BARRYMORE: Act II: Gray silk dress, underskirt, 1 pair green shoes, petticoat, hoop, fan, 1 wig, 1 pearl brooch with pearl in center, Louis XIV; 1 necklace, Louis XIV; 1 drop, Louis XIV; 1 ring from Miss Mable.

## "BERKELEY SQUARE"

### MUSIC PLOT

## MUSIC USED DURING SHOW AND IN PIT

Overture: Merry Wives of Windsor, Nicolay; Pastel, Paradis.

Between Scenes in First Act: Morgen, Strauss.

First Act Intermission: Berenice, Handel; German Dances, Nell Gwyn.

Second Act Intermision: Pastel, Paradis; Gavotte from "Iphigenin en Aulide," Von Gluck; Bouree, J. L. Krebs; Dance of the Sylphs, Von Gluck.

Out March: Pastel, Paradis.


Stage Music (Off Stage Left):
  1. Gavotte, Louis XIII, Published by Carl Fisher, No. 1126.
  2. Pastel, Paradis.
  3. Minuet in E Flat, Mozart. Published by Carl Fisher, No. 1665.
  4. Pavaue Louis XIV, Brissou. Published by Carl Fisher.

## "BERKELEY SQUARE"

## PUBLICITY THROUGH YOUR LOCAL PAPERS

The press can be an immense help in giving publicity to your productions. In the belief that the best reviews from the New York and London papers are always interesting to local audiences, and in order to assist you, we are printing below several excerpts from those reviews.

To these we have also added a number of suggested press notes which may be used either as they stand or changed to suit your own ideas and submitted to the local press.

—"Berkeley Square" is the finest play of the season—a play that casts a spell."—*J. Brooks Atkinson, "New York Times."*

"If you plan to see only one play this year, go to 'Berkeley Square.' If your budget provides two evenings in the theatre, see it twice."—*Heywood Brown, "Evening Telegram."*

" 'Berkeley Square' is a play as rare in theme as it is exquisite of treatment.—It soars to high wit and original beauty."—*Gilbert Gabriel, "New York American."*

"This is something to cheer about.—'Berkeley Square' is something to see and adore."—*Walter Winchell, "Daily Mirror."*

—"Unusual in flavor and rich in entertainment—deserves the attention of every playgoer who wants to buy an evening of complete beguilement."—*John Anderson, "Evening Journal."*

—"Enchanted its first American audience—a high born play, whose patrician quality was enhanced by the excellence of its performance."—*Percy Hammond, "Herald-Tribune."*

"It is a thing of beauty in the theatre.—It is Leslie Howard who turns 'Berkeley Square' into one of the high spots of the season."—*Robert Garland, "Evening Telegram."*

—"There is magic in the theme—a good love story—first rate comedy."—*Robert Littell, "The World."*

—"A play which is fascinating and tender and witty—it is pure enchantment."—*Gilbert Seldes, "Evening Graphic."*

"It is a tender, fanciful and amusing romance."—*John Mason Brown, "Evening Post."*

—"A beauty that lays over it like sunshine—such a play as will drive the truer sentimentalists into ecstacies of joy."—*Burns Mantle, "Daily News."*

—"A play of imaginative delicacy and charm; of wit and of romance.—One of the most completely satisfactory plays now available."—*Richard Lockridge, "Evening Sun."*

"This love story of a present-day American, who is unceremoniously thrust into the bewigged and powdered life of Eighteenth Century London, and an English girl, who has been dead more than a hundred years before his birth, is, in its poetic, fantastic way, as touching and beautiful a romantic episode as the current theatre offers. Amid all the justified enthusiasm for the adult intellectual qualities and the fascinating metaphysical conception of time that distinguish "Berkeley Square" and make it the most important play of the season, there has been too

little said for the work's enormously moving emo-
tional values."—*Richard Watts, Jr., "Herald-Tribune."*

"There is magic in this play, enough to set it
apart from the common traffic of the theatre, and
to send dreams scudding in the wake of dreams.
Therefore, first of all, let us welcome and rejoice in
it, for magic is very rare."—*"London (England)
Times."*

"Something of a recognition as well as a revival
of one of the most beautiful comedies of our time
happened at the Lyric last night over the production
of—'Berkeley    Square.'"—*"London    (England)
Morning Post."*

—"An excellent play, with a brilliant central theme
firmly handled and worked out with simplicity and
truth."—*"London (England) Daily Telegraph."*

"Love scenes exquisitely written——"—*"London
(England) Express."*

"Play of singular imagination and beauty."—*"London (England) Daily Mail."*

## REGARDING "BERKELEY SQUARE"

"Berkeley Square" suffered many vicissitudes before it reached the goal at which it was aimed, production in New York. Its author, John L. Balderston, London correspondent of "The World," dis-
plays annoyance when his work is called an "English
play." "Berkeley Square," he says, was written with
a view to New York presentation and hawked about
here before any London manager ever saw it. But
New York would have none of it, and the three or
four other managements who might have been able
to cast a play that presented so many difficulties were
not interested.

All this was in the Autumn of 1925, and while
Mr. Balderston was in Egypt covering the Tut-ankh-

Amen proceedings, a donkey toiled up the Valley of the Kings carrying a small Arab who bore a telegram from London. Alec Rea, the first manager to whom "Berkeley Square" was offered there, had accepted it within twenty-four hours, and the first production consequently took place at the St. Martin's Theatre, where the piece ran through the season of 1926-7.

The opening night, Mr. Balderston says, was rather disastrous—"it was that horrible thing, a succès d'estime"—a result due more to faults in the play than anything else. The general theatre-going public was bewildered, and it was only Rea's faith in "Berkeley Square" that kept it going at the start. It built up a public for itself, slowly, and after the last performance the audience refused to leave the theatre for twenty minutes.

Meanwhile, late in 1925, before the London production, Jed Harris, then unknown to fame, had bought the play for New York. He wanted drastic revisions and Mr. Balderston, meanwhile, with the assistance of J. C. Squire, had been rewriting the play as it was being performed. Mrs. Balderston acted as emissary between London and New York. Mr. Harris saw the play in London, but his contemplated production fell through because he could not get any one of three actors for the leading part and declared that he knew of no fourth actor who could play it.

Meanwhile, several American managements had shown interest in the play as a result of its London run, but the author declined all proposals, as he had become convinced that Mr. Harris was right in his view that the part of Peter Standish was beyond the powers of the various candidates put forward. Eighteen months ago Leslie Howard got the script, not without difficulty, and cabled Mr. Balderston in London for the rights. The reply was an immediate and eager affirmative.

Gilbert Miller and Howard put the play on for eight weeks at the Lyric in London last March as a tryout for New York. Although a revival, it built itself after Lent into such a success that several theatres were offered after the lease on the Lyric expired, and tempting touring proposals were made. In the last weeks of the second London run the play did better business than ever in its history, and on the closing night there was again a remarkable demonstration from the audience, largely made up of people who had been to "Berkeley Square" several times before. But there were other plans afoot, and the Messrs. Miller and Howard abandoned the play to the English repertoire companies, who promptly fell upon it and have since produced it everywhere.

As presented in New York now, "Berkeley Square" is unaltered from the English production of last Spring, excepting that Margalo Gillmore has taken the place of Jean Forbes-Robertson as the heroine, and in several respects the cast has been strengthened.

## DRAMA IN THE ENGLISH MANNER

The best plays of the last five or six years have been, for the most part, written in a major key. Pieces like "What Price Glory," "They Knew What They Wanted," and "Hell Bent for Heaven" were founded upon passion and violence. So too, of course, were those of Eugene O'Neill, and the American stage was distinguished from that of England or France by the bold directness with which it attacked the problems set by life in the twentieth century. Sometimes, indeed, it has seemed as though it were only here that the younger playwrights had kept their nerve—that those abroad were too afraid of being ridiculous to risk much, and that they took refuge in a delicate ingenuity from the dangers incurred by any one who strives to be important.

Personally, I have always preferred our own method. It seemed to accomplish much and to promise more; for while skill can be acquired, the achievement of a playful technique marks the end of a development, and a school of writers which has learned how to avoid the main issue is not likely to learn much more. But I must confess that this year even our playwrights and producers have chosen the minor mood, and that with the solitary exception of the "Criminal Code" no drama has attempted to reach any high seriousness. Such outstanding importations as "Rope's End" and "Many Waters" belong distinctly to the category of stunt plays. So, too, does "Candle Light," and even Mr. Hopkins turned from the grimness of last year's "Machinal" to the delightful but purely artificial extravaganza of "The Commodore Marries." In "Strictly Dishonorable" we have, to be sure, one of the best native comedies seen in years, but go where you will among the theaters and you will find that the aim is not to portray passions but to achieve, through the exercise of ingenuity, either sentiment or fantasy or charm.

It was the production of "Berkeley Square" (Lyceum Theatre) which provoked these reflections, for in it we have another stunt play which leaves far behind all major emotions and plays very agreeably indeed with an ingenious fancy. Peter Standish, a young American architect, has inherited, so it seems, an old English house in which one of his ancestors had played an important role. Taking up his residence there, he discovers that he can walk back and forth through time, that he can step into the shoes of his ancestor and live the life which that man lived in the eighteenth century. He accepts the challenge of the adventure; he finds himself entering the

"Berkeley Square"

Act III, See Page 109

old drawing-room dressed in the costume of the time but still essentially himself, and he plays the game as well as he can. Much charms but much also shocks him. His knowledge of the future sometimes trips him up, but the platitudes of the nineteenth and twentieth centuries are brilliant epigrams to those around him. He dazzles a statesman by saying that the sun never sets on the British Empire, and he amazes the Duchess of Devonshire with a few epigrams culled from Oscar Wilde. But despite his success he is not really at home. Those ghosts find something terrifying in him just as he finds something unreal in them, and at last he returns to nineteen twenty-eight carrying with him nothing except the memory of a girl whom he had loved.

Told in this bare outline the story seems preposterous, and indeed it is hardly more than a challenge to the ingenuity of the author, but that challenge he meets amazingly well. The thing is done so easily, so quietly, and with so little machinery that it is as convincing as it needs to be. One is dancing perpetually upon eggs, but the eggs never break and the suspense, the sense of a mystery not to be taken quite seriously, never fails. It is light, airy, piquant, and it is played, as it would have to be, almost faultlessly by Leslie Howard, who manages somehow to suggest the delighted bewilderment of the young hero who must appear to be at home in surroundings utterly strange. "Berkeley Square" was written by an American—John Balderston—who has been long resident abroad, and if it were not for his attitude toward his American hero one would swear that the play was English. It is a delightful evening's entertainment. It is novel, expert, intelligent, and ingenious.

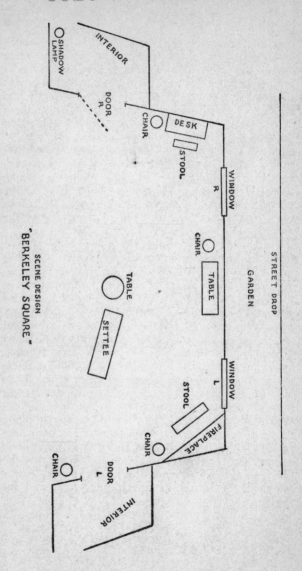

SCENE DESIGN
"BERKELEY SQUARE"